Jan

/28

How to Handle a Narcissist

How to Handle a Narcissist

Understanding and Dealing with a Range of
Narcissistic Personalities

Theresa Jackson

First published in 2017

Copyright © 2017 Theresa Jackson

All rights reserved.
ISBN: 9781521339978

Stay up to date with the latest books, special offers, and exclusive content from Theresa Jackson by following her on Goodreads, Amazon, iTunes, Barnes and Noble or Kobo.

CONTENTS

How to Use This Book

"How to Handle a Narcissist" takes a human approach to narcissism theory, combining cutting edge research, literature and discussion from academia with real, solid case studies and personal perspectives from those who have been affected first hand. The book is split into four sections, the first looking at what narcissism is and understanding the vast array of narcissistic behaviors, including healthy and extreme narcissism.

The second section is made up of stories- what other people have experienced at the hands of narcissistic people at different points in the spectrum, and how they have dealt with it. We'll also peek into the mind of the narcissist by applying the research from experts to real-life scenarios.

The third section looks at taking control, including how to cut off or limit your contact with narcissists, how to take your power back, and whether you should seek a continuing relationship with the narcissist. This section is accompanied by a complimentary workbook "Stepping Away from a Narcissist" which can be downloaded from my website, theresa-jackson.com.

.

The final section looks at how to assess the situation for greater insight into the narcissist in question, and help you plan what to do. These are mainly guided exercises, with an objective approach.

Introduction

Research has revealed how much misinformation abounds about narcissism. Public perception of the subject is a hotbed of mismatching and oversimplified ideas; with a conflicting sense of what "healthy" self-enhancement is and what is not.

Much of the misguided rhetoric published online takes a black and white approach, as though narcissism is a pure and straight forward "label," rather than a range of healthy and unhealthy reactions and behaviors, triggered in *98% of people* (including you, it is highly likely). These behaviors are present in varying intensities, for varying amounts of the time. Reactions depend not only on seemingly permanent, underlying thought- processes, but on what's going on in life, right now (and recently), that might be aggravating usually dormant self-esteem issues.

Narcissism exists on a spectrum from low levels to high. Some narcissism is healthy and is part of our normal responses to having our ego threatened, allowing us to maintain our sense of self without suffering from crushing shame and a sense of defeat. At the top of the scale is the personality disorder known as narcissistic personality disorder (NPD) characterized by a haughty sense of superiority, an inflated sense of importance and a deep need for admiration.

This book takes a more nuanced approach to the narcissistic scale. We won't simply be talking about how to deal with those that are diagnosable with NPD, but also about many narcissistic people who fit lower down on the spectrum and are relatable to most people. We'll attempt to decipher how narcissistic the person you are dealing with is, give you a better understanding of their thoughts, feelings and motivations, and help you determine whether you should cut them out of your life, or "manage" them to a greater or lesser extent.

In some cases, you might find it would be better for your wellbeing to continue a more limited relationship with them. Whether to cut off from a narcissistic mother, for example, is a hugely important decision that affects you for the rest of your life. You may have a narcissistic mother that is not diagnosable with NPD (for example, not overwhelmed with narcissistic responses most of the time, nor fitting most of the diagnostic criteria), but does display frequent damaging narcissistic behaviors that have severely impacted your "sense of safety" and trust in your relationship.

Here I will share examples of those who have found contentment by managing and restructuring the paradigm of their relationships with narcissistic people who are non-abusive. We have case studies from other people who have found themselves contemplating the decision of whether to cut off from their narcissistic mothers, and I'll be taking an even deeper dive into the complex relationship with narcissistic parents in my next book "Narcissistic Mothers and Fathers: How to Limit the Damage."

Feeling angry, humiliated, or as though you want to help or change narcissistic people is only natural. This can be incredibly tough to come to terms with. This book focuses only on what you can do for yourself, including managing the boundaries of your relationship, and asserting yourself as an independent person in your own right. If you are interested in helping, changing, or even if you are feeling vengeful toward a narcissist, I urge you to proceed with caution. I'll be looking at the complicated world of what happens when people try and interfere with the narcissistic personality in my book: "Changing, Helping or Hurting a Narcissist: Can you make a difference?"

The main priority of everyone surrounding a highly narcissistic person is to ensure that they are looking after themselves, maintaining their own mental and physical health and wellbeing, before looking after the narcissist. The narcissist's well-being should never take priority over anyone else's, whatever attempts they make to manipulate others into looking after their needs before their own. Similarly, to how we're instructed to fix our own oxygen masks before helping anyone else on a plane, you must especially remember this approach when dealing with narcissistic entitlement. If this can only be achieved by cutting contact, then this may be a route you need to take.

In the case of psychological, emotional, or physical abuse, the answer of what to do next is simple. Nobody should be in a position where they are suffering abuse at the hands of another, and if this is the case for you, stopping the abuse by leaving the situation is the only course of action to take. If you can't leave, this book will help you to explore your options about how to manage the situation, to put yourself in a more protected position where your well-being is less on the line.

You may find that a narcissistic person in your life is not abusing you but is negatively impacting you in some other way- through guilt, manipulation, bullying- or simply using you for their own means. We'll start this book by helping you assess how narcissistic the person is, so you can begin to understand their thinking.

Section 1

Understanding the Narcissistic Person

-1-

What is Narcissism?

There are two main schools of thought and research into narcissism, the first dealing with people who cross over the diagnostic threshold into the clinical disorder of Narcissistic Personality Disorder (NPD) and the second which treats narcissism as a scale onto which we all fit.

This book is intended to help anyone with a narcissistic person in their life, whatever their position on the scale, not just for dealing with the four percent of people who cross over into the extremities of NPD.

Because we all sit on the narcissism scale, we'll be taking more of a human approach to this subject, attempting to understand narcissism, including the good, the bad, and the ugly. That way, the methods you choose for handling difficult situations in the future can be grounded in empathy and come from a place of positive intentions. This can ensure that you look after your own best interests first, without inflicting unnecessary harm on an easily wounded individual.

The Narcissistic Scale

Most of what is written about narcissism focuses solely on narcissistic traits as being negative. Like most things in life, the situation is somewhat more complicated than this.

According to Professor of Psychological and Brain Sciences, Susan Whitbourne, of the University of Massachusetts Amherst, one of the myths surrounding narcissism is that you are "either a narcissist or not." People equate a whole person with the condition of narcissism simply by using the word "narcissist." In this way, society makes the mistake of not recognizing that people have narcissistic tendencies to different degrees and develop personality features to counter their narcissistic tendencies.

One thought-provoking study by Professor of Psychology, Jonathan Freeman, of the University of London, found that 98% of people exhibit narcissistically inflated self-perceptions of their own qualities, from how 'nice' they perceive themselves to be, to how well they drive, how attractive they are and how good they were at leading others.

Most people display narcissistic traits in a balanced manner, mostly at appropriate times, either as part of a confident yet *empathetic* character, or as a defense reaction to a genuine threat. Narcissistic qualities are necessary to gain approval, reassurance and love, as well as to protect the ego and self-identity from perceived criticism, scorn or defeat that could lead to crippling shame or a sense of defeat. However, life events, stress and interactions with different people will cause fluctuating levels of narcissism in many people that are not clinical narcissists.

What about those who don't exhibit enough narcissism? It is a commonly held misconception that narcissistic traits are entirely bad. However, many experts agree that some narcissistic traits are positive. Dr Craig Malkin, a Lecturer at Harvard Medical School, has been investigating narcissism as a scale of "self-enhancement" and has classified three main groups on the scale.

He found two distinct groups in addition to the widely discussed "bad" narcissists. People who never, or rarely, feel special and focus too much on others at the expense of themselves have been coined "Echoists." This demonstrates the need for self-confidence and a positive, healthy self-regard. "Healthy narcissists" range from mid to very high levels on the self-enhancement scale, but are empathic, confident and ambitious, yet able to offer and accept help.

It is the individuals that sit high up on the self-enhancement scale and additionally show predominantly manipulative, approval-seeking and argumentative behaviors, and who suffer from fluctuating self-esteem that are potentially damaging to those around them. This group was coined "extreme narcissists" by Dr Malkin.

Egocentric individuals, as well as those that are sensitive to criticism, display stronger, more frequent and less reasonable negative narcissistic responses that make them increasingly difficult to be around or maintain relationships with. They may be hypervigilant, often perceiving insults and threats where there are none, due to deep-rooted insecurity or a genuine sense of superiority.

If these tendencies reach high enough levels, an individual can be medically diagnosed with narcissistic personality disorder (NPD). NPD is characterized by a grandiose sense of self-importance, a lack of empathy, need for excessive admiration, and a sense of entitlement.

If the tendencies come and go, or are only prompted some of the time, or are only present at low levels, a diagnosis is unlikely. This in no way means that the narcissistic individual is acting in a way that is good for those around them. It also doesn't mean that people around them must accept their behavior or allow it to affect their lives negatively.

-2-

Scoring Narcissistic Traits

I'm making the presumption that as you've bought this book, you have an individual in mind that you know well enough to answer some questions on their personality and estimate a standardized narcissism score. In this chapter we will be looking at two assessment methods. First, we're going to be using the original version of the most widely used scoring system, the Narcissistic Personality Inventory (NPI), which is a 40-item checklist adapted from the clinical criteria for NPD, so that it is applicable to the general population, and not just those with a disorder. In addition, I've provided an adapted version of the inventory that allows you to split the score into positive and negative features and allows for questions where neither option fits.

I'm also going to challenge you to score yourself as well! During my research, it has become clear that some experts believe narcissists frequently flock together, and you might be interested to find out whether you also score highly for these traits.

The Narcissistic Personality Inventory

Instructions: *Here you'll find a list of 40 opposing choices in pairs. For each pair choose A or B that you believe* **best matches the person in question's opinion of themselves** *(even if it's not a perfect fit). Answer all questions for the most accurate result*

1.	A	○	I have a natural talent for influencing people.
	B	○	I am not good at influencing people.
2.	A	○	Modesty doesn't become me.
	B	○	I am essentially a modest person.
3.	A	○	I would do almost anything on a dare.
	B	○	I tend to be a fairly cautious person.
4.	A	○	When people compliment me I sometimes get embarrassed.
	B	○	I know that I am good because everybody keeps telling me so.
5.	A	○	The thought of ruling the world frightens the hell out of me.
	B	○	If I ruled the world it would be a better place.
6.	A	○	I can usually talk my way out of anything.

	B	○	I try to accept the consequences of my behavior.
7.	A	○	I prefer to blend in with the crowd.
	B	○	I like to be the center of attention.
8.	A	○	I will be a success.
	B	○	I am not too concerned about success.
9.	A	○	I am no better or worse than most people.
	B	○	I think I am a special person.
10.	A	○	I am not sure if I would make a good leader.
	B	○	I see myself as a good leader.
11.	A	○	I am assertive.
	B	○	I wish I were more assertive.
12.	A	○	I like to have authority over other people.
	B	○	I don't mind following orders.
13.	A	○	I find it easy to manipulate people.
	B	○	I don't like it when I find myself manipulating people.
14.	A	○	I insist upon getting the respect that is due me.
	B	○	I usually get the respect that I deserve.
15.	A	○	I don't particularly like to show off my body.

	B	⊘	I like to show off my body.
16.	A	⊘	I can read people like a book.
	B	○	People are sometimes hard to understand.
17.	A	○	If I feel competent I am willing to take responsibility for making decisions.
	B	⊘	I like to take responsibility for making decisions.
18.	A	○	I just want to be reasonably happy.
	B	⊘	I want to amount to something in the eyes of the world.
19.	A	○	My body is nothing special.
	B	○	I like to look at my body.
20.	A	○	I try not to be a show off.
	B	⊘	I will usually show off if I get the chance.
21.	A	⊘	I always know what I am doing.
	B	○	Sometimes I am not sure of what I am doing.
22.	A	○	I sometimes depend on people to get things done.
	B	⊘	I rarely depend on anyone else to get things done.
23.	A	○	Sometimes I tell good stories.
	B	⊘	Everybody likes to hear my stories.
24.	A	⊘	I expect a great deal from other people.

	B	○	I like to do things for other people.
25.	A	○	I will never be satisfied until I get all that I deserve.
	B	○	I take my satisfactions as they come.
26.	A	○	Compliments embarrass me.
	B	○	I like to be complimented.
27.	A	○	I have a strong will to power.
	B	○	Power for its own sake doesn't interest me.
28.	A	○	I don't care about new fads and fashions.
	B	○	I like to start new fads and fashions.
29.	A	○	I like to look at myself in the mirror.
	B	○	I am not particularly interested in looking at myself in the mirror.
30.	A	○	I really like to be the center of attention.
	B	○	It makes me uncomfortable to be the center of attention.
31.	A	○	I can live my life in any way I want to.
	B	○	People can't always live their lives in terms of what they want.
32.	A	○	Being an authority doesn't mean that much to me.
	B	○	People always seem to recognize my authority.
33.	A	○	I would prefer to be a leader.

	B	○ It makes little difference to me whether I am a leader or not.
34.	A	○ I am going to be a great person.
	B	○ I hope I am going to be successful.
35.	A	○ People sometimes believe what I tell them.
	B	○ I can make anybody believe anything I want them to.
36.	A	○ I am a born leader.
	B	○ Leadership is a quality that takes a long time to develop.
37.	A	○ I wish somebody would someday write my biography.
	B	○ I don't like people to pry into my life for any reason.
38.	A	○ I get upset when people don't notice how I look when I go out in public.
	B	○ I don't mind blending into the crowd when I go out in public.
39	A	○ I am more capable than other people.
	B	○ There is a lot that I can learn from other people.
40.	A	○ I am much like everybody else.
	B	○ I am an extraordinary person.

Assess the results!

Add together 1 point for each A answer for these questions: 1, 2, 3, 6, 8, 11, 12, 13, 14, 16, 21, 24, 25, 27, 29, 30, 31, 33, 34, 36, 37, 38, 39.

Add 1 point for each B answer for these questions: 4, 5, 7, 9, 10, 15, 17, 18, 19, 20, 22, 23, 26, 28, 32, 35, 40.

Total Score: _____
(Please split out the total score into positive and negative traits in the next section)

The overall score should be between 0 and 40.

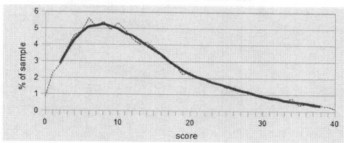

Source: Personality-testing.info

The bell curve peaks at just under 10- meaning this is the most common score, but the average (mean), across the whole spectrum is around 15. Different populations vary with college students averaging at 15.6, adults at 15.3 and celebrities at 17. With various positive and negative features of narcissism on the rise due to fashion and cultural trends the average has also been increasing. But how do we know whether this is a bad thing or not?

Classically, there has been no definition on the NPI of whether a trait is considered "good" or "bad," all have been considered equally- in line with the negative connotations of all narcissistic traits- even those such as leadership and confidence. Also, considering that for many of the questions, many people report that neither of the options can be considered a suitable answer, the reliability of the score is called into question, perhaps even being affected by self-assessment bias such as whether an individual has a realistic self-image, or not. Being forced to choose between two opposite poles, when neither is the reality can only reduce the accuracy of a score. We will consider how to take a more balanced approach in the next section.

"Healthy" and Negative Attitudes

Considering Dr. Malkin's work, which demonstrates that healthy levels of narcissism and self-enhancement are necessary, with a low level of self-enhancement being detrimental to our wellbeing and success, it is helpful to distinguish between positive ("healthy") and negative traits. This can help to prevent the discouragement of traits that should be encouraged and attempt to understand the contradictory messages surrounding narcissism.

In the following adapted version of the NPI, a middle ground has been offered for questions that are entirely polar, making a representative choice for many average people impossible. Other questions remain an A/B choice.

The scoring system splits the inventory into "healthy" traits and the classically interpreted "negative" narcissistic traits. Traits related to feelings of superiority, entitlement and exploitative have been assigned as negative, as these are inherently derogatory and harmful towards others. Traits associated with confidence, leadership, self-sufficiency, authority, body-pride/exhibitionism, and vanity have been split into groups depending on whether they show modesty, healthy narcissism, or extreme narcissism. This has been performed in line with Dr Malkin's definition of a "healthy" narcissist (showing confidence, empathy and ambition) and extreme narcissists (showing manipulation, approval-seeking, controlling and argumentative behaviors).

Instructions: *Here you'll find a list of 40 statement groups. For each group, choose statement A, B or C that you believe* **best matches the person in question's opinion of themselves.** *Answer all questions for the most accurate result.*

1.	A	I have a natural talent for influencing people.
	B	I am not good at influencing people.
	C	I can influence people on some subjects, if I feel strongly
2.	A	Modesty doesn't become me.
	B	I am essentially a modest person.
	C	I am often modest, but in some areas of specialty in which I do well I am confident and happy to self-promote
3.	A	I would do almost anything on a dare.
	B	I tend to be a fairly cautious person.
	C	I take risks sometimes, so long as they're not too risky

4.	A	○	When people compliment me I sometimes get embarrassed.
	B	○	I know that I am good because everybody keeps telling me so.
	C	○	I can accept compliments well if I think they seem genuine
5.	A	○	The thought of ruling the world frightens the hell out of me.
	B	○	If I ruled the world it would be a better place.
	C	○	Ruling the world would be difficult but I hope I would do well
6.	A	○	I can usually talk my way out of anything.
	B	○	I try to accept the consequences of my behavior.
	C		n/a
7.	A	○	I prefer to blend in with the crowd.
	B	○	I like to be the center of attention.
	C	○	I like to get attention at times, and at other times I like to blend in
8.	A	○	I will be a success.
	B	○	I am not too concerned about success.
	C	○	I will try to be a success
9.	A	○	I am no better or worse than most people.
	B	○	I think I am a special person.

	C	○	I am a special person in some ways, and so are many other people
10.	A	○	I am not sure if I would make a good leader.
	B	○	I see myself as a good leader.
	C	○	n/a
11.	A	○	I am assertive.
	B	○	I wish I were more assertive.
	C	○	Sometimes I am assertive, at other times I let things go
12.	A	○	I like to have authority over other people.
	B	⊙	I don't mind following orders.
	C	○	I like to have authority, but I also don't mind following orders
13.	A	○	I find it easy to manipulate people.
	B	○	I don't like it when I find myself manipulating people.
	C	○	n/a
14.	A	○	I insist upon getting the respect that is due me.
	B	○	I usually get the respect that I deserve.
	C	○	I like to feel respected, but can let it go if I am not
15.	A	○	I don't particularly like to show off my body.
	B	○	I like to show off my body.

	C	○ Sometimes I like to show off my body, and other times I do not
16.	A	○ I can read people like a book.
	B	⦿ People are sometimes hard to understand.
	C	○ I am quite good at reading people
17.	A	○ If I feel competent I am willing to take responsibility for making decisions.
	B	○ I like to take responsibility for making decisions.
	C	○ I like to make decisions but am sometimes unwilling if I don't feel prepared
18.	A	○ I just want to be reasonably happy.
	B	○ I want to amount to something in the eyes of the world.
	C	○ I want to be reasonably happy and successful at achieving my goals
19.	A	○ My body is nothing special.
	B	○ I like to look at my body.
	C	○ I am happy with my body.
20.	A	○ I try not to be a show off.
	B	○ I will usually show off if I get the chance.
		○ Sometimes I show off but no more than anyone else.

21.	A	○	I always know what I am doing.
	B	○	Sometimes I am not sure of what I am doing.
	C	⊙	I often feel confident with what I am doing
22.	A	○	I sometimes depend on people to get things done.
	B	○	I rarely depend on anyone else to get things done.
	C	○	n/a
23.	A	○	Sometimes I tell good stories.
	B	○	Everybody likes to hear my stories.
	C	○	n/a
24.	A	○	I expect a great deal from other people.
	B	○	I like to do things for other people.
	C	○	I like to do things for others and receive things from other people too
25.	A	○	I will never be satisfied until I get all that I deserve.
	B	○	I take my satisfactions as they come.
		○	I strive to achieve goals, which gives me satisfaction
26.	A	⊙	Compliments embarrass me.
	B	○	I like to be complimented.
	C	○	Genuine compliments are welcome, flattery is not

27.	A	○ I have a strong will to power.
	B	○ Power for its own sake doesn't interest me.
	C	○ I prefer some power and influence to none but it is not a strong drive to achieve power for power's sake
28.	A	○ I don't care about new fads and fashions.
	B	○ I like to start new fads and fashions.
	C	○ I sometimes follow fads and fashions if I like them
29.	A	○ I like to look at myself in the mirror.
	B	○ I am not particularly interested in looking at myself in the mirror.
	C	○ Sometimes, when I have made a special effort, I like to look at myself in the mirror
30.	A	○ I really like to be the center of attention.
	B	○ It makes me uncomfortable to be the center of attention.
	C	○ Being the centre of attention does not bother me but I don't need it or crave it
31.	A	○ I can live my life in any way I want to.
	B	○ People can't always live their lives in terms of what they want.
	C	○ I hope to live how I would like
32.	A	○ Being an authority doesn't mean that much to me.

	B	○ People always seem to recognize my authority.
	C	○ I enjoy being an authority in some areas
33.	A	○ I would prefer to be a leader.
	B	○ It makes little difference to me whether I am a leader or not.
	C	○ n/a
34.	A	○ I am going to be a great person.
	B	○ I hope I am going to be successful.
	C	○ n/a
35.	A	○ People sometimes believe what I tell them.
	B	○ I can make anybody believe anything I want them to.
	C	○ n/a
36.	A	○ I am a born leader.
	B	○ Leadership is a quality that takes a long time to develop.
	C	○ I have become quite a good leader, or I think I would be good at it
37.	A	○ I wish somebody would someday write my biography.
	B	○ I don't like people to pry into my life for any reason.
	C	○ My biography might be interesting one day
38.	A	○ I get upset when people don't notice how I look when I go out in public.

	B	○ I don't mind blending into the crowd when I go out in public.
	C	○ n/a
39	A	○ I am more capable than other people.
	B	○ There is a lot that I can learn from other people.
	C	○ I have some areas of expertise, and I can learn from other people's areas of expertise
40.	A	○ I am much like everybody else.
	B	○ I am an extraordinary person.
	C	○ I am special in my own blend of talents and attributes, as is everyone else

Assess the Score

For each question look up your answer and assign 1 point to either healthy narcissism, unhealthy, or 0 points for not narcissistic, using the table on the following pages.

	Score 1	Score 2	Score 3
1.	B	C	A
2.	B	C	A
3.	B	C	A
4.	A	C, B	
5.	A	C, B	
6.	B		A
7.	A	C	B
8.	B	A, C	
9.	B	C	A
10.	A	B	
11.	B	A, C	
12.	B	C	A
13.	B		A
14.	B	C	A
15.	A	C	B
16.	B	C, A	
17.	A	B, C	
18.	A	C	B
19.	A	B, C	
20.	A	C	B

21.	B	C	A
22.	A		B
23.	A		B
24.	B	C	A
25.	B	C	A
26.	A	C	B
27.	B	C	A
28.	A	C	B
29.	B	C	A
30.	B	C	A
31.	B	C	A
32.	A	C	B
33.	B	A	
34.	B		A
35.	A		B
36.	B	C	A
37.	B	C, A	
38.	B		A
39.	B	C	A
40.	A	C	B

Score 1: Modesty score:____ (typical score ranges from 5 to 17, average 11)

A modesty trait exhibits no narcissism but shows an area of low self-enhancement. Behavior may potentially be positive and altruistic, but could also potentially be a sign of self-deprecation, low self-esteem, or lack of confidence. On the other hand, it may also be an objective and realistic approach that has been learned due to negative feedback or failure in some areas of life. It is normal to exhibit some of these in some areas of life, perhaps areas that an individual has repeatedly attempted to master but has been unable to do so.

Score 2: Healthy narcissism score:____ (typical score ranges from 11 to 29, average 21)

A healthy narcissistic trait may show positive self-belief, confidence, empathy, ambition, leadership, inspiration, objectivity, and balance. It is normal to exhibit these in many areas of life. For example, research has shown that most people over-estimate their abilities to drive well, their levels of altruism, intelligence and how good-looking they are, rating themselves as above average in most of these areas. Men tend to over-estimate themselves more highly than women, particularly when it comes to rating their own physical attractiveness, whereas women tend to have a more realistic idea about themselves in this area. Believing oneself to be "better than average" in many areas of life is part of the human condition, and a propels us forwards towards success with confidence, in these areas.

Score 3: Unhealthy narcissism score:____ (typical score ranges from 3 to 10, average 6)

Unhealthy narcissistic traits are exhibited through excessive attention seeking, superiority, haughtiness, derision, delusion, manipulation, grandiosity and a need to maintain narcissistic supply. It is normal to exhibit some of these in limited areas of life, perhaps areas that are particularly sensitive for an individual.

High levels of healthy narcissism can be considered positive, whereas higher levels of unhealthy narcissism or modesty can be considered concerning. Most people have a blend of all three, (areas of righteous confidence, no-confidence, and deluded confidence), that are displayed at various times alongside attitudes of humility or superiority, empathy or callousness, and honesty or manipulation.

-3-

Healthy and Extreme Narcissism

Healthy Narcissism

Confidence, charisma or appreciation of your actual talents/attributes without these attributes leading you to believing you are a superior person to others, are all positive traits, encouraged by most societies. An ability to lead and inspire are similarly positive traits. These traits can be described as healthy narcissism.

Many confident, out-going, successful people have high levels of healthy narcissism and self-enhancement, believing in themselves and putting themselves forward rather than shrinking in the face of challenges and attention. But these positive aspirational mindsets lack the belief that they are "better" than anyone else, or the will to act in a superior manner. Confidence and self-belief are healthy, but over confidence and believing your positive attributes make you better than other people, crosses from healthy to extreme narcissism. Confidence and self-belief do not make healthy narcissists un-empathic or manipulative. These healthy traits should not be confused with unhealthy or damaging narcissistic traits, as often seems to be the case in many online materials.

This lines up well with Dr Malkin's finding that 1% of people score very highly on healthy narcissism, and very low on extreme narcissism- individuals who light up the room and inspire others rather than undermining them. They view both themselves and others through a rose-tinted, optimistic lens, and encourage and inspire others rather than feeling threatened by their success.

Extreme Narcissism

Narcissistic Supply, Attention and Superiority

Positive feedback, attention and approval as rewards for doing well or being a certain way are enjoyed by everyone to a degree, but those who score highly for narcissism (both healthy and extreme) increasingly revel in it. People with extreme narcissism start to need it to maintain their sense of wellbeing- protecting themselves from coming down from their high, like an alcoholic will avoid being sober. Some also have a wavering sense of self-esteem dating back prior to the development of the dependency.

For everyone, love and praise create pleasurable feelings as they release dopamine- the brain's reward neurotransmitter. For people with underlying low self-esteem, as well as those that have problems regulating their dopamine levels, this experience can be particularly attractive. The pleasurable rush acts as a "tonic" to soothe underlying feelings of pain from feeling negatively about themselves.

Dopamine is also released when an individual discovers that they have a talent and can be successful in some way, or when they discover an activity or attribute that brings them praise or positive attention (such as being attractive, being good at sport, being academically talented or achieving goals at work). For most people, this results in the pursuit and development of skills and interests and is how healthy narcissism develops. Many truly confident and kind people become attracted to attention and limelight, reveling in performing for others- think comedians or talk show hosts such as Ellen DeGeneres or James Corden. These people are probably not hiding extreme narcissism; they're likely to just be friendly, outgoing and confident.

In individuals who initially felt defected, bad, or "low value," the positive feelings gained from attention and approval can lead to a habit of seeking out similar experiences repetitively to an unhealthy degree, maintaining their ego by ritualistically inflating it, gaining attention for being good, attractive, successful or intelligent. This is called "narcissistic supply," with the term "supply" being used in a similar way when talking about addictive drugs. Not only this but having used or released a large amount of dopamine during a "rush" of narcissistic supply, some individuals may then be vulnerable to a "crash," in a similar but less extreme way to how a cocaine addict may experience a high and then a "come down" when their dopamine levels spike and then fall.

This can result in rapid cycling of moods, and a constant seeking out of more supply to maintain the high. Side effects of plummeting dopamine levels include feelings of depression, anxiety and irritability. These cycling moods do nothing for the extreme narcissist's sense of self-esteem, particularly if low self-esteem pre-existed before the dependency. Feelings of guilt and shame may then exacerbate the cycle- propelling the extreme narcissist to remain inflated and enter a state of denial about what it is like to be around them when they crash, and how they then interact with the world.

Those who score highly for extreme narcissism can become competitive for the limited "supply" that they receive from those around them. If we imagine the attention of one individual as a small package of "drugs," we can see how this works. The amount of drug is limited, and the addict wants much of it for themselves. Extreme narcissistic people are frequently threatened and jealous of those around them, reacting viciously to maintain their supply and their sense of "goodness," "correctness" or superiority. They may use many forms of manipulation to get as much narcissistic supply as they can, whilst justifying it to themselves.

Experiences that cause the release of dopamine- such as drinking alcohol, taking drugs, having sex, or smoking cigarettes- are known to be potentially addictive for this reason. The pleasurable release of dopamine and inflated self-esteem from narcissistic supply, offers an escape from naturally low dopamine levels, or the pain of feeling as though the narcissist is defective or "bad" in some way.

At higher points along the spectrum, the constant need for validation and praise can reach unquenchable levels, where no amount of "supply" is enough to maintain the narcissist's inflated sense of self.

Perceived criticism or mistakes made by a vulnerable narcissist can result in an almost instantaneous and crippling return to this state of low self-esteem. However, when under threat our cognitive defenses may be extremely adept at protecting us from experiencing this type of pain.

Narcissistic defense responses may kick in to block out the threat and "save" the narcissist from facing what, to others, would constitute taking responsibility for their actions. To those that are lower on the narcissistic scale, this shows up as the more narcissistic party becoming defensive and refusing to take responsibility for their hurtful words and actions. They may attack in response to any perceived insult or threat to their self-esteem. To the individual at hand, however, this choice between taking responsibility and remaining defensive may well be the difference between staying afloat and functional and breaking down completely.

Can Extreme Narcissists Love?

The claim that narcissistic people "cannot love" is an over-simplified and negative view that does not look at the technicalities of what is happening between narcissistic highs and defenses. This idea forgets the nuances and complications of human beings.

Claiming that all narcissistic mothers are not able to love their children, or that a narcissistic spouse is not able to love their partner is black and white, unrealistic thinking.

So, what's going on? People who have extreme narcissism traits are frequently inflating themselves to feel good, defending themselves against "crashes," and protecting their egos against injury, meaning they may think of themselves a great deal, without much time to think of others.

Whether people who demonstrate a high frequency of extreme narcissistic tendencies can feel love in the typical sense, is likely to depend on the individual. They can certainly undergo the same "infatuation" response as the rest of us, releasing and becoming "hooked" on dopamine and feeling as though they are falling in love. Ironically, being in love may feel like a beautiful experience involving a cherished and idolized partner, but it has been shown to be inherently selfish. People that are in love seek to serve their own emotional needs, rather than predominantly empathizing with their partners' (those on the receiving end of unrequited love have been shown to be more capable of empathizing with the "in love" party, than the person who is in love is able to empathize with them).

Whether feelings of being in love from the extreme narcissists' point of view resemble healthier individual's experiences is open to discussion. Whether these feelings progress further to feelings of romantic love, and then on to a sense of attachment that is comparable to healthier individuals are also not conclusive and is also likely to vary from person to person.

Defense against emotional pain.

Most narcissistic people – lower down the scale, who spend much of their time "untriggered" – may be perfectly capable of feeling love and empathy during those times. Extreme narcissistic people may, however, fear falling in love because they may view themselves as unworthy or incapable. This can cause them to dread the pain and vulnerability love would bring when their partner eventually left or betrayed them.

However, just because they fear it, deny it, or have little time to dedicate to it, does not mean that they are invulnerable to it. They may not be able to express it in healthy ways. If a feeling of vulnerability from falling in love is anxiety-provoking, they may seek to assuage this feeling by indulging in infidelity, belittling their partner, forming multiple attachments to lower the strength of the primary attachment, or attempt to lower the value of their partner in some way.

Love and compassion for others cannot take priority at times when narcissistic reactions are taking place. The chance to gain supply or the need to defend against a threat to the ego must first diminish before loving feelings can emerge or be expressed. In cases where these activities are a full-time pursuit, love and empathy may never happen.

Defense against emotional pain, sits very high on the brain's automatic priorities list. Love sits lower in the brain's list of automated priorities. Which doesn't mean that love is valued less by our logical brains or value systems. It means that our brains' automated responses (which are subconscious and unconscious) move first to protect us from emotional pain, before considering

43

higher notions such as love and empathy.

Read more about real life examples of how love is expressed in narcissistic relationships in section 2.

Extreme Narcissists Who Use Their Lovers

The higher up the scale a person is, the more likely that the narcissist is viewing other people as objects to be used for their pleasure. They may not be able to be considerate or loving and may only be there to take what they can. Often, they will only give back if it helps them to take some more.

Some narcissists have a pattern of idolizing their lovers and friends, suddenly seeing their faults, devaluing and discarding them without a second thought. Often, they'll have a new lover or friend that they have been waiting to switch their attention to. If this has happened to you, you'll know how devastating and confusing this can be, as the narcissist can swing from being the center of your world, to not seeming to care that you exist.

In some cases, however, they may also retain past lovers, friends and family in the wings in case they are needed, chasing them and reeling them back in if they think they are losing their interest. Keeping in contact can be useful as they might need sex or attention later when their options for supply are few.

Subtypes of Extreme Narcissist

Over the years there's been much debate over the various types of extreme or unhealthy narcissists that exist. According to Professor

Whitbourne, a further myth (commonly believed), is that narcissists are similar, or the same, as one another.

In reality, even within subcategories of narcissism, important individual variations exist. Essentially, all individuals are unique, and don't fit neatly into perfect categories or groups. We might see an individual as a unique recipe of traits.

Masterson's subtypes of narcissism were defined in 1993 as the exhibitionist (corresponding to the grandiose narcissist defined within the DSM) and the closet narcissist.

The closet narcissist possesses negative narcissistic qualities such as a sense of superiority, entitlement and varying self-esteem, but hides these under a false exterior of modesty. On the other hand, exhibitionist narcissists will tend to be the "life and soul" of the party, as their healthy narcissistic traits are paraded for show, and their unhealthy traits are hidden to the outside world.

Exhibitionist narcissists, like healthy narcissists, tend to be charismatic, charming, and well liked. It is frequently the case that those in the periphery of their lives think that they are exceptional individuals. From the outside, friends and colleagues would have a very difficult time perceiving the narcissist as being harmful or insecure. Those close to the narcissist, however, are often more clued up to the fact that something could be wrong, perhaps privy to abuse or manipulation firsthand.

Further subtypes of narcissist have been defined as:

Unprincipled or malignant (antisocial, fraudulent, exploitative)

Amorous or sexual (including attention seeking behaviors such as exhibitionism, womanizing, being seductive and sex addiction)

Compensatory (passive aggressive and avoidant)
Elitist (superior, entitled, obsessed with status symbols and keeping up appearances)

Acquired situational (develops after childhood in response to wealth, success or fame)

Destructive (frequent and persistent presence of extreme narcissism traits but at lower levels than NPD)

Amorous or Sexual =
1. exhibitionism
2. womanizing
3. Being seductive
4. Sex addiction

Section 2:

Stories of Narcissists

"While it is wise to learn from experience, it is wiser to learn from the experience of others" Rick Warren

-4-

Real Narcissistic People

Narcissistic people frequently don't fit into neat boxes, or display exact, prescribed behaviors. They are rarely black and white villains as hype would have us believe. Diagnostic criteria are useful for identifying a general sense of how someone may think and act in the world, but labels garnered from a few questions on a list will never capture the complexities of a human being.

As an example of how straight forward, or confusing attempting to decipher someone's mindset can be, I have two case studies, one straight forward, the other complex.

Valerie

Valerie is a relatively straight forward case of high level, extreme narcissism, with an estimated healthy narcissism score of 10, extreme score of 27 and a modesty score of 3. She fits mostly into the elitist category, as her main driver is "becoming something in the eyes of the world," making her life appear perfect to anyone who will listen, and exaggerating her career, lifestyle and financial achievements. She avoids social media, preferring to remain mysterious and aloof rather than compete with "inferior" individuals who would make her question her own sense of achievement.

Valerie is extremely vulnerable to criticism, failure, or a perceived lack of love and support. She manipulates anyone she wants something from and would fill with narcissistic rage at inappropriate times when she feels her superiority and entitlement was under threat. Sometimes she has loving feelings towards others, is loved and can be incredibly sweet and caring. Her family successfully manages their relationship with her but deal with frequent challenges involving paranoia and bouts of aggression.

Jim, on the other hand is a complicated puzzle- a bundle of contradictions. By his own admission he spends most of his time feeling very little emotion or empathy for others, is a frequent liar, and manipulates people for sex (all of these are typical narcissist *and* psychopath behaviors). He carefully sets up his life so that he is surrounded by a string of infatuated women that he can call upon when he needs to indulge himself. He is determined to be invulnerable emotionally and has a strong drive to succeed professionally, in the eyes of the world. This in itself is healthy, except for the underlying self-esteem issues.

Despite being manipulative, Jim often refuses to take the easy road. There is something honest in the way he holds out his guiltiest secrets to warn the women he has hooked and "save them" from himself. He tries to make them see how "terrible" he is at "being a human being." He doesn't want to hurt them but continues to manipulate them so that he can use them as he wishes. At times, he is childlike- pouring affection onto animals. Animals are a safe outlet for his affections as they expect nothing more than what is being offered and have no emotional expectations that will lead them to be disappointed. Showing affection to a partner always comes with too high a price tag of expectations, inevitable failure, and shame.

Jim has a diagnosis of ADHD, which accounts for his constant need for stimulation, impulsivity, sexual promiscuity, as well as a need for novelty and excitement. He used to worry that he may be a psychopath.

Until recently, Jim seemed determined to keep soldiering down his own blinkered pathway, toward what lonely end, we can't say. But since integrating and acclimatizing with a new group of warm and welcoming friends, he appears to have "grown" as a person and be looking to grow further. His conscience is moving in line with that of his friends and he seems to be open to their influence.

So, is Jim a narcissist? Essentially, it appears he has (or had) amorous and sub-principled narcissistic traits, was ambitious to be *more* psychopathic (in order to become invulnerable) but now wishes to become more principled. His ADHD as the underlying cause of many of his issues has made it a slower process to organize his thoughts into moral values, and subsequently upholding these values has been difficult because of impulsivity issues. Difficulty adhering to his own moral code then exacerbates his self-esteem issues, leading to self-medicating narcissistic behaviors, such as seeking sex to feel better about himself.

Confused? Indeed. We can see that although some people may fit relatively neatly into a category, they may still not be a cut-and-dry villain. A label cannot possibly define someone entirely. We may have recognized someone in our lives as having narcissistic traits, and we may be on the path to understanding them and handling our relationship, but we certainly can't judge them or label them as "bad" or hopeless as much of what is written on the subject would urge us to do.

Classifications Don't Matter

So, what does all of this tell us? Can we ever truly understand someone thoroughly? There is an overlap of traits between many of the diagnostic checklists, with psychopathy, narcissism and ADHD particularly overlapping – with varying underlying causes. Whilst narcissists may or may not be aware of their motivations to a degree, they may need to engage in more self-justification, denial, or bravado to alleviate feelings of guilt, whereas a high-level psychopath may be less inclined to care.

People with NPD, and psychopaths, often have an inflated grandiose self-image, can be charming, can participate in pathological lying, manipulation, are often sexually promiscuous, and have a need for constant stimulation. One study suggests that in some psychopathic patients, this lack of empathy is a conscious decision, and empathy can be switched on or off at will in these individuals. Psychopathic individuals may have higher levels of awareness of the manipulation they are undertaking than narcissists, planning it carefully, with varying degrees of remorse.

It's also possible for people to qualify for multiple disorders, it doesn't need to be just one. Classifications and "pigeon-holes" do not always work. The human brain is a messy, complicated system, and we can't always get a perfect answer. Fitting someone "well enough" into a category that helps you understand a decent portion of their behavior, without them being a perfect fit should be enough for you to decide what is generally happening and take appropriate action.

If there is someone in your life that is causing you emotional distress or pain, whether they're narcissistic, egocentric, psychopathic or anything else, it's time to take control of your own boundaries, and your own emotional health.

At the highest level first, we're going to look at case studies from people who dealt with abusive, controlling narcissists. Before you continue to read, if you think you may be in an abusive relationship with a narcissist, please do not interpret the content of this book as meaning you should attempt to fix or take responsibility for the relationship.

Abuse is wrong, end of story. It is your right, and your responsibility to yourself to remove yourself (and any dependents) from such situations and cut all contact if this is what is better for you (and more importantly, any dependents). Never question this right, or yourself, and take whatever actions are necessary to make this happen. If you are unsure about whether what you are experiencing is abuse, please check the section "What constitutes abuse" in the final section of this book, where you can also find contacts for services that you can use to escape from abuse if you need them. In addition, an example of a "log book" entry can be found in the same section, which facilitates objective note taking on your situation, to see things more clearly.

Escaping an Abusive Thirty-Year Marriage

This is the case of Maria, who married her high school sweetheart. The couple were married for over thirty years before Maria eventually left her husband, who was an extreme, grandiose narcissist.

Extreme narcissists, like many healthy narcissists, often make great first impressions, and this includes romantically. The difference is that after four months, relationship satisfaction with extreme narcissists shows a drastic decline, and not simply in line with that of an average person's relationship or the typical end of the "honeymoon" period. Adult narcissists are not happy people, and they tend to make their partners unhappy too.

Despite having two children together and a long marriage, Maria's husband Jeff, never "grew out of" his selfish and narcissistic behaviors, as Maria continuously hoped he would. After thirty years of being portrayed as the "bad guy," suffering every put down imaginable, she eventually realized enough was enough. Jeff was reacting badly to aging and his abuse was spiraling out of control. She recalls the feeling of desperately needing to get out, or risk entirely losing herself.

Their relationship began with Maria as the idealized apple of Jeff's eye. He had been dating Maria's good friend Jody before he abruptly ended the relationship and turned his attention to her. She could do no wrong. He blasted her with praise, affection, gifts and dedications and the pair were the golden couple of their school.

The honeymoon period lasted for about a year into their relationship before Jeff started to show a different side to his character, devaluing Maria and putting her down constantly. Nothing seemed to make him happy. Maria went from being perfect to being able to do no right. There was not enough praise, adulation or encouragement that she could give that would bring back the Jeff that she fell in love with or stabilize his mood swings.

Maria started to wonder if Jeff was the right man for her after all. And suddenly, everything changed. Jeff became his old self again over night. He took her for dinner, told her she was beautiful and whisked her away for a week at the beach. It seemed as though her prayers had been answered. It was not long afterwards that Jeff proposed on a moonlit cruise, after a candlelit dinner and an evening of elegant dancing. Maria gleefully accepted. Looking back, she cannot count the number of times she heard this story repeated. To Jeff, it was a badge of honor, letting everyone know what an incredible husband and spouse he was. Retelling the story became a way of securing admiration and narcissistic supply.

Looking back, she reluctantly admits that his behavior had improved in the run up to the proposal, allowing Jeff to idealize himself as the perfect boyfriend and partner. All of it was a part of the story that he told himself and other people, to keep his ego inflated. To him, he was the perfect man, and he constantly told Maria how lucky she was, requiring constant thanks for anything he did for her.

On the run up to the wedding, Jeff reveled in the attention and could not have been more publicly devoted to his fiancée. He never missed a chance to tell his family stories of what she had said or done, how beautiful and successful she was, and how much he adored her.

Behind closed doors, however, was a completely different Jeff. Maria was accused of having sex with her co-workers, berated for putting on weight, and told exactly what to wear. If she didn't thank him enough or praise him enough, she was selfish and inconsiderate.

As soon as they were married, the verbal abuse became worse. He started to accuse Maria of being a lesbian and having multiple affairs. If she developed friendships, he would strongly disapprove and accuse her friends of being lesbians. After scoring a verbal victory against her, particularly if he had reduced her to tears, Jeff would walk around whistling as though he didn't have a care in the world.

It was not long before Jeff was back in touch with Jody, sending emails through secret accounts, and making calls with a secret cell phone. To Jody, Maria was a loveless and uncaring spouse. When Maria discovered his secret accounts, she could not believe the lies that he told about her, or how he twisted everything that happened.

Jeff and Jody spent five years lying, sneaking and meeting in strange places for sex behind their spouses' backs. When Maria confronted him, he begged for her forgiveness, and despite being devastated, Maria agreed to forgive him. On the same evening, Jeff insisted that Maria accompany him to a family engagement, where he put on a show of the perfect marriage and the perfect family man, as though nothing had happened. Of course, he expected Maria to play along with his show.

Years passed, and Maria became used to his verbal abuse and tyranny, as though it were a normal part of life. The couple tried counselling and therapy, where Jeff would talk at length about what a "good man" he was. He was unable to tolerate criticism, which eventually led to him refusing to return to the sessions. He started the therapy with a list of ultimatums including Maria admitting that she was a lesbian and forcing their youngest daughter to move out immediately. As soon as the therapist suggested that Jeff were responsible for being insensitive or abusive, Jeff found multiple reasons to discredit her and refused to return.

Sadly, when their daughter was a teenager, she developed an eating disorder and was diagnosed with bipolar disorder. Jeff would come home late at night and attack her verbally, aiming his aggression at her weak spots- body image, being "weird" or "crazy" and her sense of self-worth. He told her she should lose some weight, told her she was "going crazy again," and when his own daughter responded with comments like "maybe I'd be better off dead" he would reply "don't let me stop you."

Eventually enough was enough. Maria saw the damage that Jeff was doing to their daughter and decided she had to leave. Her therapist advised her that Jeff's behavior was not normal. She finally felt validated as though she were not the bad guy, and as though she was not going mad. Still, it took time and courage to build up the strength of mind and the details of a plan to get away from him.

When she told him that she intended to leave, Jeff laughed in Maria's face and told her that she had no one and nowhere to go. When she packed up and left for her sister's house, he begged her to stay, at one point physically restraining her before yo-yoing back and forth between telling her how worthless she was and begging her not to go.

Maria left anyway. It was difficult for a very long time, and she nearly turned back and went home at several points along the road to recovery. Jeff was a popular figure in their small town, chairing their high school PTA and a prominent member of their church. She was no longer just the "bad guy" at home, but also a "bad guy" in town and in her community. But despite many people who were never going to see through the glossy narcissistic screen that Jeff had built up for years, surprisingly there were a few people who could see through it. Maria had a gentle and quiet integrity, and for some people, this cast doubt on the lies and rumors that Jeff spewed about her amongst their joint friends and family.

Maria and their daughters now live their lives with a smaller group of friends, and with the love and support of her sister and extended family. They live without the feeling that they are evil, neglectful or worthless. And it is a decision that she thanks God every day that she took. Jeff still contacts her occasionally, professing his love for her in poetic idealistic terms, before making some accusatory comment about how terribly she had treated him. But she sees it for what it is- emotional blackmail from someone trying to milk her for attention and trying to make her accept blame to feel less guilty themselves.

Lessons from Maria

We can see that despite Maria having tried for thirty years to make the marriage a success, Jeff was not able to change his abusive behaviors, which simply became exacerbated as his insecurity regarding his age grew. His mindset was too extreme, and he was unable to take an alternative to an egocentric viewpoint.

During this thirty-year period, Maria suffered immensely, and their daughter developed an eating disorder as well as bipolar disorder, which may very well have been avoided had she acted at an earlier point. Although hindsight allows us to see with clarity, this case study is a good illustration of how remaining in an abusive situation rarely ends well and is likely to only get worse.

An Estranged Mother's Death

Jan's story is troubling, involving liberation from a haunting childhood only when her mother passes away, and has been previously featured in my book "Loss of a Parent" about adult grief when parents pass away.

Jan found out that her estranged mother had died by text message at the age of 26. She finished up her shift as a waitress in a cloudy fog, not telling any of her colleagues the news, before meeting her husband after work. She hadn't spoken to her mother in two years, after years of painful issues in their relationship. Prior to their estrangement they had been having regular calls, trying to make things work, attempting to salvage their wreck of a relationship. As an only child, Jan was all her mother really had left. Her mother had been trying her best to be a better mother.

Despite adamantly denying that she had done anything wrong, something seemed to hit home that her daughter had woken up to the name calling, competition, and attempts to control her life. Her mother had started trying to live up to her own self-image, and the image that her friends and family thought her to be. That was all that Jan really wanted. For her mother to be like the mother that everyone thought she was.

For years, she had desperately wanted her supposedly perfect mother to stay perfect after the curtain call, when her aunts and uncles weren't around. But inevitably when the rest of the family went home- and they were alone- instead she was subjected to selfish manipulation, competitive jibes and angry insults. Her mother couldn't help but put her own needs far above those of her daughter.

One day on the phone during a petty argument, her mother calling her an idiot, and it rang true against all the other times she'd been called worthless, a wimp, a coward, a little bitch, a whiner or useless. She remembered being told that she'd never amount to anything after a successful audition for the local church choir, which filled her mother with envy. Minutes later her mother had been bragging on the telephone about the achievement, as though nothing had happened at all.

It was a tiny, insignificant insult, but it ripped at her heart and sent her spirally towards self-loathing and despair. *If your own mother thinks of you like that,* she reasoned, *then surely it must be true.* As it turned out this small insignificant insult was to be the last breath of their relationship.

When Jan hung up the phone, she broke down in tears, wondering what to do, knowing that something had to change. She couldn't withstand the constant threat of crippling pain at any moment, and years of injustice and denial within the family. She realized in that moment that it was pointless to hope for more, and all she could do was walk away. And not just from her mother, but from the whole tainted family unit. A unit that would always side against her, and firmly stand with her abuser.

She had suffered years of denial of her abuse at the hands of toxic friends and family who only recognized that her mother was perfect, but that weren't witness to the daily verbal abuse, twisted perception, and emotional manipulation that seemed so out of the realms of possibility to them. It made Jan question her own sanity and wonder if she was making a mountain out of a molehill, she wondered if the situation really was as bad as she felt it was.

For the following two years, Jan refused to have a relationship with her mother. Holidays were particularly difficult, but she assuaged the guilt by sending her a card and a gift and spending the time with friends. Denying her mother's phone calls and visits had been difficult, but in the long term she felt it would be for the best.

When she died, Jan felt guilty that the death of her mother was in some way a release from the insults and gnawing feeling of unworthiness that had been bottling up inside. Years later, she was able to embrace her mother's tainted love for her, and her reciprocal love for her mother, without feeling shame or guilt. She understood her mother's family history and could see that the toxicity into which her mother had been born had sadly tainted their relationship to an incredibly painful degree, and this had not been her mother's fault either.

Jan had slowly pieced together the story of her mother's upbringing over the years, and the cause of her narcissistic personality. As the middle child in a family of six siblings she had been somewhat neglected by her parents and very much overlooked in favor of her siblings. She worked hard at school, but it wasn't until she discovered a talent for singing that she began to receive attention for her voice, above all other things. Her grandfather had been a chaotic mix of fun, frustration and drunken rage, often berating her mother and sending her away to live with relatives.

Feeling unloved, Jan's mother had worked hard to always be perfect, but still felt unloved underneath. She never had anything of her own and was fiercely protective of what was hers when she got it. This understanding of where her competitive, controlling and narcissistic rage came from helped Jan to see her mother through new eyes and empathize with her rather than hold onto the negativity of the past.

Lessons from Jan

Whether or not you agree with Jan's drastic decision to cut off from her mother, we can see from Jan's story that an understanding of the narcissistic person's history can help us to come to terms with their subsequent treatment of us. Whilst it does not excuse their behavior, we may be able to empathize with them in some way, and so process our painful feelings more effectively.

Recently, a psychiatric study found that the most significant consequence of narcissism – especially when controlling for other psychiatric symptoms- was the suffering of people close to them. Jan found that even a small amount of contact with her mother resulted in significant suffering, and so she decided to take control of her borders and go no contact, to make it stop.

Three Years of Control

Claire and Dom's three-year relationship started well and took several months before it became abusive. Small red flags surfaced early on, but Claire turned a blind eye because she was in love, as well as being in mourning for her father, who she lost a few weeks after they had begun seeing each other.

Outwardly, Dom was intelligent and charming, but with insecurities about his self-worth, coupled with OCD and anxiety. His vulnerable narcissism meant that he felt the need to prove himself socially, academically and professionally.

The first warning sign that appeared was that Dom was not only willing to manipulate other people, but that he carefully planned how to do so, and enjoyed it. He referred to himself as "Anansi the Trickster God" – the god of lies and deceit- and shortly after they got together, Dom got a tattoo of a spider on his shoulder to represent his God-like status and ability to deceive and manipulate anyone. In a moment of honesty, he admitted to manufacturing a scene to manipulate and win over Claire's best friend, who he arranged to "catch him" in the act of "gazing" at Claire. With love in his eyes, he purposely confessed how incredible he thought she was, with the simple purpose of getting her on side. Later, when Claire shared her concerns with her best friend that something wasn't right, her best friend rejected them outright, angrily telling her that she didn't know how lucky she was.

Another indicator of a personality imbalance was that Dom would intensely loath various people, including close friends and family. Particularly, he hated his mother who had been generally disapproving during his childhood, putting pressure on him to perform perfectly and disparaging him harshly for not meeting the highest of standards. This had led to the development of a great deal of self-loathing. He quickly became determined that Claire should agree with every opinion, every decision and fantasy, to provide the approval that he had so desperately craved from his mother.

After a few months, his character seemed to split into two. On the one hand he was intelligent, witty and charming- and on the other he was cruel, strange and abusive. The manipulation became physical, when one evening he pinned Claire to a wall by her neck. From that point during their relationship he would constantly pin her to the floor of their apartment whenever he felt like it, as a "joke." He broke her makeup, cut the ear off a teddy bear and constantly berated her for being a "know-all" whenever she questioned him or voiced a differing opinion. Claire started to think that it would be easier simply to agree to everything that he said.

In a bizarre twist which almost seemed to be a confession, Dom described how he planned to write a novel in which a "secretly gay man" marries a woman who is "just attractive enough" and spends the rest of his life convincing her that she is insane. Shortly after this revelation, Dom revealed that he had latent homosexual feelings himself, hinting that the book was somewhat autobiographical, but refusing to speak any more on the subject, leaving Claire confused and worried.

Over the first year of their relationship, Claire resisted being dominated and controlled, and the dynamic within the couple was fraught with conflict. Dom began taking things to an extreme level to "win" their battles. He manipulated their friends and families to his advantage to make them see him as the "perfect" partner, and her as unworthy and ungrateful. Slowly, Clare was isolated from her sources of support. His efforts to break her will and independence of thought intensified until she felt she was losing her mind. He seemed to be instigating a long-term strategy of convincing her that she was crazy, and that everyone in their lives could see it but her.

Claire wondered if she was mad, as he insisted, wondering if everything was her fault. But she felt as though she had no proof to make up her mind. She remembered that she had been objective and strong at one time but found that under the pressure of the relationship she was suffering from frequent and substantial memory loss. No matter how hard she tried, she couldn't seem to remember the cause or content of the intense, all-encompassing arguments that seemed to occur on an almost daily basis.

It was only after Claire decided to secretly keep notes on things that were said during arguments that it dawned on her how badly she was being verbally and psychologically abused. With a log book of comments, she finally saw objectively.

The log book could not lie, and it could not forget. She read in black and white that Dom would tell her that she was pathetic. That she would die alone, that nobody cared about her. That she knew it was true and that's why she was crying. That she had gotten a C grade average in college and still thought she was so clever. He would tell her to f*** off, that she was a psycho bitch, and blame her for their arguments. Insist the relationship had wasted their lives.

He needed excessive praise for every small task he did, but it never seemed to be enough. He would pin her down on the floor by her shoulders, and not allow her to move, accusing her of assault if she retaliated to get him off her.

In between these angry attacks, he would swing to apologize and grovel, beg forgiveness, explain that what he'd said had come from the "darkest depths of his soul" before mocking her "crocodile tears" moments later. He would insist through clenched teeth that "everyone we know knows that all of our **** problems are all your **** fault, don't they Claire? They all **** know it," telling her if their friends could see her, they'd all call her a psycho bitch. This, she finally realized, had been his tactic all along. To get everyone onto his side and cast her as the crazy "bad guy."

He would tell her he was leaving her and would never see her again "and I'm so f****g happy about it.", "When I said nobody cares about you and that you would die alone? I was reflecting the truth (evident I think)."

It took Claire another year to eventually break free and realize that no matter how many counseling sessions he agreed to go to, he would never stop the rollercoaster of anxiety and abuse. She suffered a mental breakdown, depression, and even an out of body experience before she eventually walked away. Perhaps with someone less independent, she thought (still blaming herself), he might have a better relationship.

For years, she continued to believe that she had something to be ashamed of for walking away from the turbulent and abusive relationship. That she had somehow "ruined his life" by leaving him, rather than finally putting her wellbeing first. She really believed she was the bad guy.

Years later, she realizes that resisting manipulation and mind control, and looking after her sanity was nothing to feel guilty about. Dom continued to contact her for many years, bragging about his achievements and making attempts to put her down whilst at the same time hinting that their relationship had meant a great deal to him.

Out of a misplaced sense of duty she responded, until a friend pointed out that she was under no obligation to reply and that she had no reason to feel any guilt if she chose to cut contact. With immense relief she found comfort in knowing she had no further duty towards him, and that no one could reasonably expect her to be responsive towards him. Being happy and not looking back has been a decision that took many years to reach.

Lessons from Claire

From this story, we can see that narcissists don't always target people who are easily broken or manipulated but can also be attracted to people they find challenging to "break." In the same way that challenging situations provide stimulation for some people, so they do for narcissists.

We see how difficult it can be to be objective when in the midst of an intense relationship. Manipulation is often insidious and can sneak up slowly. Usually it's not something that can be reasoned with or worked out logically, it comes from the expression of deep-seated issues and an interaction that won't simply stop through arguments and discussions.

Using a tool, such as a log book, to record the events and nature of words used during arguments, can help a confused mind see more clearly in the long run. You'll find one in the "Assessing the situation more clearly" section. This can really help to overcome the excuses that tend to occur in abusive relationships, where one partner starts to make excuses for the escalating behavior of the other. Holding a narcissistic person accountable for their unacceptable behavior can prove extremely difficult, which may add to the cycle of excusing bad behavior, simply for want of an easier life.

Recovering from a Manager with NPD

Shirley's account of her boss with narcissistic personality disorder (NPD) aligns well with studies into how narcissism reveals itself in the workplace. Typically, extreme narcissists will make a good first impression on their colleagues, but after three weeks will typically be seen as untrustworthy.

Shirley describes how after two months with her new boss, the trouble started when he got really upset over a little issue, losing his temper unexpectedly and lashing out at his two subordinates close by. Shirley's manager's mood always seemed to be changing. Cheerful -to the point of being on a high- one third of the time, "low" one third of the time, with the remaining third somewhere in the middle.

Later in the year, during a typical meeting- with seven other employees in the room- her manager got annoyed by a small insignificant event and flung a pile of papers at one of her colleagues. Shocked, all eyes turned to the manager, who seemed to be the most shocked of all. He frightened himself so much in losing control that he immediately switched to courteous deference and fawning. From hostile, to gratuitously friendly in a matter of seconds, as though he were an observer to his own bad behavior and although in denial of the problem, aware that he might be uncovered if he didn't make up for and cover up the incident.

The manager went on later that year to fire the top performer on his team, to prevent them from becoming a serious threat. This had been because their excellent work had taken the spotlight away from him, meaning the threat had to be eliminated.

At any one time there seemed to be an immediate "ring of fire" of people disappointing him and receiving the brunt of his fury. If you managed to stay at a safe enough distance, life could remain somewhat stable. But once inside, life changed forever, and you were never again on the outside or safe from harm or criticism. Her manager would seemingly fall in love with someone, assigning them a golden halo and endless unwarranted responsibilities. When they would inevitably fail, the hero would be vilified, before returning to a position of neutrality or boring non-existence if they rode out the storm for long enough.

Sometime after she broke away from her manager, he called her, and she let it run to voicemail. He asked for her to return his call, but she didn't. Instead, sometime later he attempted to provoke a response and messaged a close friend of hers to say that she had "lost credibility." She attributes this to paranoia, with an unsuccessful attempt to woo her generally being followed up by an attack to bolster his ego.

Lessons from Shirley

Shirley describes how having had a manager under the influence of NPD, she has a lot of sympathy for those in relationships with similar people. She sees NPD as an addiction like alcoholism. An alcoholic is not in control of himself- his addiction is in control. A person with NPD is addicted to Narcissistic supply. With alcoholism, you run to a bottle to get your next fix, for narcissistic supply the addict runs to a person for a fix, and if they are refused, like a drunk refused at a bar, hostility is often what follows.

Despite this viewpoint coming from a non-professional, the validity of the argument aligns well with expert opinion. When Shirley woke up to the fact that her manager had NPD, she kept reminding herself that she wasn't dealing with a person half of the time, she was dealing with the addiction itself, and that the person in question had been "kidnapped."

During "come downs," where no narcissistic supply was being received or "highs" when there was plenty, they were unable to control themselves reasonably. These thoughts helped her remain empathetic and understanding of what she was dealing with, yet strong in her dealings with her manager. She resisted being sucked in to the "ring of fire" and remained on the periphery, creating enough distance to prevent herself from being sucked into the danger zone.

Narcissistic Families

Adam cut off from his egocentric, paranoid and power-focused mother for a year, and barely spoke with his brother or sister whilst coming to terms with his damaging experience in their narcissistic family unit. He won't allow himself to be shamed into being the "lowest of the low" or a "disgusting human being" simply because he has a mind of his own. And given the choice between this position and walking away, he would gladly walk away.

Following a significant break of several years of very limited family involvement, he found that adapting his relationship to his family- rather than cutting off from them entirely- has been a positive solution all round. As adults, the family dynamic became less intense, no one in the family was extreme enough in their narcissistic traits to prevent this from happening. With distance, their higher selves- with warm personalities and humor -were able to shine through the narcissistic paranoia and power struggles.

His siblings and mother were perfectly capable of being enjoyable, caring and reasonable most of the time, so long as the mother remained unthreatened and all-knowing as the head of the family.

Adam slowly and carefully created a decent and regular relationship of phone and text message contact, with occasional in-person visits, that were as non-threatening as possible. Occasionally sending a joke, a picture or a "How are you? Remember this..." maintaining this for some years. By keeping them at more of a distance, whilst still expressing affection and interest in them, he was able to feel satisfied and protected from the drastic and harsh reality of having no family at all.

Even though the relationships are more distant than he would ideally like, he finds the distance keeps them all safe from having boundaries intruded upon, prevents him from simply being "an audience" for their pleasure, and halts strange power dynamics and paranoia before it starts.

The months following the initial break off were the most difficult part of the change, after everything had come to a head. One Christmas day, at lunch, the family had been sitting to eat, and his mother was telling a story about how one of his cousins had been very rude to her- demanding to know where her Christmas present was, as everyone else had received one when she was in the bathroom. As a snapshot in time, the incident was indeed very rude. But Adam knew that the back story between the two sides of the family was increasingly tense in recent years.

The previous year, at the funeral of his grandmother, Adam's mother had led the decision that only her brothers and sisters- and not their children- should be allowed up to the coffin to say goodbye during the ceremony. This caused a lot of upset, particularly for the "rude cousin's" brother, Joe – who had a special connection with his grandmother. She'd always had time for him, and if he was ever in trouble or going through a difficult stage, she never wrote him off as the "bad kid," like other people might.

Sadly, Joe decided not to go to the funeral in protest, with the tension between the two sides of the family growing hugely (it was in fact an extension of the tension between the eldest and the youngest sister from a large family, and their subsequent families). Adam's mother had always spoken derogatorily about her sister as a matter of principle. Adam, however, through Facebook, had been given an insight into the fact that his aunt was not the monster she had been made out to be but was in fact a sweet and doting mother. It could be seen that the incident, was the "rude cousin's" way of voicing the tension between them. A way of standing up for her brother against a perceived injustice.

As Adam's mother indignantly discussed the offensive incident, Adam- unwisely- piped up with the comment "Perhaps this isn't about the gift? Maybe it's more about other things than it is about the present? Maybe this is about the funeral arrangements where Joe didn't go to the funeral?"

Adam's stepfather, (someone who is highly diplomatic, easy going and prefers not to rock the boat) immediately piped up with his adamant agreement "Yes, that could be it, that makes sense," he nodded, eager to reduce the tensions between the family parties. The stepfather speaking up was a rare occurrence, and it didn't last for long. Adam's mother sat in stunned silence at the apparently offensive suggestion that there could be another way of looking at things and seemed wounded at what she saw as a betrayal against her rule of thought.

His sister, also at the table, immediately launched into a rage, storming from the table and shouting at Adam that he could sometimes be "too reasonable." Which, rather than an insult, he considered to be more of a compliment. Adam, sank into a pit of shame and despair, not allowed to question or speak his views within his own family for fear of rejection- as it had been since he had been able to speak. His mother- a teacher- had ironically raised him to study hard, think critically and be highly academic, but expected him to tow the line and never disagree with her. A confusing lesson indeed!

Later that day, as he lay sobbing upstairs, his stepfather checked on his wellbeing. Adam decided to leave rather than sit in a well of shame and self-loathing. The next day he received a text message from his mother simply telling him to change his address, as a letter had arrived for him at her house. He responded with a careful explanation about how emotionally irresponsible and neglectful he felt she had been over the years and (predictably) received nothing back.

Adam and his mother didn't speak for over a year. Despite loving her son, his mother was incapable of questioning herself or her lack of emotional skills. She presented a "united front" of "it's us against you" from the family- for the first time in thirty years sending a joint birthday card to him from herself and his sister as if to say, "You didn't break us," and beginning a new tradition of having family parties each Christmas that Adam was not invited to or told about. It seemed she was purposely isolating him as though he were a trouble-maker, when ironically he had attempted to be a voice of reason and compromise. This type of behavior could be seen echoed in other family affairs, with "divide and conquer" being one of his mother's most used techniques to maintain her rule.

All of these efforts to manipulate and control perceptions within the family arose from a "too reasonable" comment that was intended to be helpful, that perhaps his mother might consider an objective point of view rather than degrade the reputation of another family member without considering their point of view. The comment had resulted in a strong reaction from his sister who wanted to maintain the status quo at that moment, and a strong narcissistic reaction and the need to deny and attack from his mother. Adam, although hurt by the "game playing," took solace elsewhere, as he had since he was a child.

As a child, Adam had resorted to imaginary friends for solace when he was young, not allowed to play with the other children in the neighborhood and unwilling to sit silently in the living room with his family being "shushed" every evening as his mother tried to watch the television. When he was old enough to leave the house and make friends independently, he avoided going home at all costs. Shy at first, his friends quickly realized that Adam was a decent, honest and funny member of the group and he finally came into his own. He realized that he had two identities: at home the assigned role as "weird" black sheep of the family, that he had gained for daring to question his mother, suppressed, silent and withdrawn. Amongst his friends he was the sweet funny one who didn't like his friends smoking, and stood up for people against racism or bullying.

After the incident at Christmas, as an adult, Adam grew much closer to his grandmother, as she genuinely seemed to love him and care about him, taking an interest in his life, his wellbeing and activities. It gave him a sense of what motherly love was supposed to be- constant, interested, stable and affectionate. More importantly, it was interactive. The discussion went in both directions. Although his grandmother (like most people) considered herself to be in the right most of the time, all hell would not break lose at the slightest suggestion that she might be wrong about something, and the relationship was not a dictatorship. He also enjoyed seeing how his grandmother maintained relationships with others, calling, writing and taking an interest in their lives in a way his mother never did.

Prior to this, his impression of his grandmother had been clouded by his mother's opinion of her – that she was full of mind games, controlling and annoying (as his mother seemed to think of many females).

He began to piece together all of the family rifts, divisions and isolations within the family unit that his mother had been involved in. Firstly, his mother had banned his father's parents from the family home over Christmas and never missed an opportunity to try and turn his father against his parents completely.

At another point, years later, she had been convinced that his stepfather's sister was trying to hack into her eBay account, simply because she didn't understand that a computer uses Autofill settings to suggest previously used login details. As funny as this may sound, he realized that since that incident his mother had indeed successfully managed to isolate her and mock her within the family for being "too girly" to the degree that neither he nor his siblings accepted any contact from her (as though being girly were a crime).

Looking back, Adam realized there had been a nasty and damaging family rift between his father's live-in girlfriend and Adam and his siblings that was greatly contributed to by advice from their mother. The ridge was never bridged.

Adam had at one point befriended his stepsister, who had been a pre-teen when their parents had gotten married, and yet who Adam barely knew, as his mother had decided not to include her in the family, for fear of losing control. At dinner one evening his stepsister had commented of their parents that "You could wait for a year and never be invited over" to which Adam had to sadly agree. He felt vindicated that he had not been imagining the bizarre neglect and division within the "family" that seemed to step from his mother's egocentric nature.

One thing that he realized when piecing events together was that his mother particularly did not like women and naturally distrusted any feminine, attractive or girly qualities. She felt particularly threatened by females who were perceived to be competition for influence over the man in her life. This list included Adam's grandmother and aunt, and his stepfather's sister. The exception to the rule was his stepfather's mother, who was bookish, straightforward and conservative so that Adam's mother felt no threat from her.

Adam went to stay with his grandmother for Christmas from then on. Somewhat forgotten by the family and having neither of her children to look after her, she finally felt that somebody cared about her too. Adam and his grandmother genuinely liked each other and cared about each other, whereas his mother seemed to care more about games. No one could interfere with their connection or take it away from Adam to isolate him- although his mother subsequently tried.

Adam's mother noticed the budding relationship between him and her ex-mother in law and interpreted it as a game. She made "counter moves" where she attempted to be the "hero," suddenly taking an interest in her ex-husband's mother that she had previously vehemently distrusted. She needed to ensure that Adam's sister was also being given "fair access" to their grandmother, and that Adam was not somehow making his sister feel cut out (a typically paranoid and pessimistic interpretation from someone undergoing a narcissistic response).

Having only ever received one phone call from Adam's mother in forty years, Adam's grandmother welcomed the sudden attention- the flowers, the picnics, the visits- short-lived as it all was, and when the spotlight inevitably moved on, she continued to maintain constant and regular loving contact with Adam.

Adam and his mother barely spoke for the following few years until he felt able to objectively explain the turmoil within the family, and how it had affected him. He was careful not to point the finger at her, never explained to her how he believed her to be highly egocentric and controlling, but he did share how he found it difficult to always bear other people's problems. Always acting as a go-between for warring family members, or a pair of ears. Enough was enough and he had had to walk away and start to look after himself for a while.

Eventually, Adam's mother realized that he was genuinely willing to walk away, rather than concede to her power games and mind control. She opened herself to meeting and lunching together, particularly because his reasonable approach made it difficult for her to refuse and still look like "the good guy." Keeping up her internal sense of being right, as well as external appearances was hugely important to her.

Initially when they met, she was always full of stories about the family, how wonderful things were without him, how heroic she was being helping various poor souls, and how much she hated her husband's sister. Stories to inspire sibling rivalry, and a sense of "it's us against you" abounded. And they hurt. But he persisted with their relationship, none the less.

Slowly, bit by bit, chipping away at her resolve to maintain an "us against you" dynamic, he refused to let her shirk her responsibility towards him as a mother. He knew she wanted to label him as a "bad guy" or "irresponsible" in some way so that she could feel justified in writing him off as a "nasty piece of work," which would allow her to not have to bother with him, whilst also maintaining her sense of being good and correct. He could not give her any fuel to enable her to do this.

He persisted to initiate occasional, loving, reasonable, and cheerful contact- not allowing her to see him as the source of any trouble. He modelled the contact on the relationship with his grandmother, and on how he had seen his ex-girlfriends had maintained healthy relationships with their parents (although admittedly it was usually the parent that instigated most of the contact, which Adam realized would never happen with his own mother).

His mother continued to have bouts of paranoia during individual lunches or occasions, and he tried his best to deal with them, but overall his stance of absolute fairness and reason could not be perceived as anything but being decent and coming from a place of integrity. Although this still makes her nervous to this day, not being able to discredit him, as time goes by, it seems she has noticed how uninterested he is in engaging in power plays.

The distance creates a sense of seriousness in his mother, whereby she and the rest of the family can see that he is willing to walk away from them if he needs to, if they treat him poorly. They also understand through the distance that he is not a threat to them. How can he be a threat if he is only occasionally present? How can they treat him badly if he is willing to walk away? To keep him in their lives- and maintain appearances in the rest of the family- they must be humanly decent and control themselves to within appropriate boundaries. They must respect him as a human being in his own right, and not as an extension of themselves, expecting him to tow any line they tell him.

Lessons from Adam
The reason "cutting off" and regrouping at more of a distance has worked in this case is because Adam's mother, the instigator of the dynamic, is not so extreme in her narcissistic traits that she is controlled by them all of the time. The family finds him challenging, as he questions the status quo of the omnipotent and controlling mother at the top of the heap, whereas the rest are willing to follow her lead to maintain peace. Adam presents an alternative, less

81

egocentric worldview, which none of them much appreciate. But as they are not entirely engulfed in narcissism and denial- they have not lost the ability to reason or be objective in the long run, when they are able to see him from a distance.

As an intelligent and logical family, they see themselves as being reasonable and ethical, and always doing the "right thing." The distance allows their relationships to be controlled by each individual, with little time for paranoia or power games to creep in.

They know he is not "playing games" as the mother previously saw it, because he has walked away for prolonged periods in the past, when their behaviors became too much. Because of this – they also know he means business. His only desire is that he simply wants to be able to have a relationship with them, preferably one which is authentic- where he can be true to himself- holding an occasionally differing opinion, and not have to cater to his mother's views, bowing to her at all times.

If he is not allowed to have this, then rather than fight and lose in a dirty, manipulative battle aimed at putting him through the emotional ringer until he concedes, he will simply withdraw, and walk away- dignity intact- until a month or two later when they can converse again about the weather, work or holidays. His sister, having taken the opposite approach of engaging in hand to hand combat on an emotional level, has been showing the emotional damage outwardly for years and gets very upset very easily.

In a situation where you are dealing with someone as paranoid, competitive, argumentative, and controlling as Adam's mother, it can be particularly important to act to high moral standards. Whilst your actions may well be interpreted in line with any model a paranoid person sees fit, making sure that you limit anything that might be perceived as interfering, manipulative or meddling is important.

Unfortunately, simply developing a relationship with an outside family member or friend – which is a positive thing- can be interpreted as a conspiracy. In this case, continuing to act reasonably, and consistently until the paranoid party lets go of the idea, is all that can be done. And if they don't, which they may not, there is nothing more you can do about it. At least you have developed a mutual support relationship with a person that is healthy.

Additionally, rather than getting involved as a diplomat in difficult family arguments, or when being asked to take sides, simply stating that you are "no longer getting involved," may be the best line of defense to prevent being stuck in the middle. Often trying to help means that others may turn around and blame you for their own arguments.

It may also be helpful to show a complete lack of interest in power, games or control. Not engaging in tit-for-tat demonstrations of how "wonderful" you are when a narcissist brags and being as straight forward and direct as possible can also help to reduce a narcissist's paranoia. If they have reason to question your motives- they probably will.

Sometimes, the situation makes Adam sad that engineering and maintaining the distance is necessary, but nowhere near as sad as if he had to entirely cut off from them, so overall, he's happy with how things are. The question for readers of this book is assessing which is better for your situation, and whether you can engineer an environment in which a family can express love for each other, at a safe and undamaging distance. You'll find a work sheet on how to unravel the layers of paranoia in narcissistic families, and how to go about creating an action plan for this in the "Assessing the situation objectively" section.

Section 3:

Taking Back Control

-5-

Techniques to Handle Narcissists

Now comes the difficult part! Deciding what to do with the narcissistic person in your life, and what the best outcome is. This can depend greatly on your individual circumstances as well as the person at hand.

Get Away

The most obvious, but by far the best piece of advice for dealing with narcissists that are not central to your life and are of no emotional significance to you is to not interact or deal with them at all. This section of the book is accompanied by a complimentary workbook "Stepping Away from a Narcissist" which can be downloaded from my website at theresa-jackson.com and aims to help you concrete your plans into actions.

Typically, extreme narcissists lack normal levels of empathy, don't pull their own weight, and tend to make the people close to them miserable within the space of a few weeks or months. They are unlikely to have a great deal of insight into their damaging behaviors and are unlikely to have an epiphany compelling them to change.

It may be tempting to try and open their eyes to the cause of their problems, help or change them, but this is far more likely to misfire with defensiveness or lead to resentment (depending on how extreme they are). According to MIT negotiation professor John Richardson when assessing a situation and considering whether to continue, never start with "How do I make this deal?" but rather "should this deal be made?" Unfortunately, with many people who score highly for extreme narcissism, the answer is no. You are unlikely to get a fair deal, and you are likely to end up less happy by keeping them in your life.

Relationships you *could* potentially cut off include not only romantic partners, friends and ex-colleagues, but also family. If you are not legally bound to remain in contact with someone – such as engaged in a business, joint ownership of property, administration of a will, or where a dependent is involved, then you have the potential to cut away if you need to.

Although it may be a very difficult consideration, none of us *must* remain in contact with anybody if the other party is causing us serious emotional damage. But taking the drastic step of cutting off- permanently- could well be something that will live with us for many years to come and should not be taken lightly.

Less drastic steps include taking a break or managing the situation. Breaks can help to gain clarity, but it depends upon the relationship at hand, and whether you deem it to be worth saving. If abuse is currently involved in the relationship, an immediate cut-off should be instigated, rather than attempting to make the best of it (see the abuse checklist in the final section).

It's important to choose the people you spend time with wisely, because humans tend to adopt the characteristics of those around them. Professor Nicholas Christakis of Yale University explains this in terms of the ripple effect, whereby altruism and meanness ripple through networks of people, and be magnified. Whatever enters your system- including the actions of your peers, colleagues and family- will affect your personality development and outlook. Surrounding yourself with good people will make you behave in more kind and empathic ways.

Avoid the Inner Circle

If you need or want to keep a narcissist in your life, it is much safer to do so at a distance, rather than as part of their inner circle- who become privy to their chaotic changes in temperament. Creating justifiable distance (but remaining warm) allows you to be a welcome part of their life without suffering so many falls from grace. They may well start to think of you quite fondly. Get too close, however, and you may become an undervalued part of the furniture, without your own identity or boundaries to respect. In addition, you are giving more opportunities for your words and actions to be misinterpreted as threats or competition, and you are far more likely to have your fingers burned.

Whist you may have identified the narcissist as a damaging individual, many people (particularly those under their control) will never be able to see the situation clearly. This can feel extremely unfair and unjust to those who can, particularly in family or romantic situations, if they are directly affected by narcissistic control, abuse or manipulation. The narcissist may be a master at making others look like "the bad guy," and may even have laid the groundwork for this future eventuality to further their control.

It is usually those people who "question" the status quo that the harmful narcissist finds most threatening, and subsequently suffer most acutely at their hands, as the narcissist feels compelled to bring them down to maintain their position. If the narcissist is a family member, particularly a parent, or a partner, this can be particularly damaging, with the victim often trained to unquestioningly agree or go along with the narcissist's opinions, to maintain their love and their favor. Those that follow receive their rewards, whilst those that question, are isolated, ridiculed and ousted, often labelled as a "black sheep," "troublesome" or "combative."

Avoid Narcissistic Injury

Sometimes, cutting the chord on a narcissistic relationship is not an option. You may feel you should at least try and continue a non-abusive relationship, in which case avoiding "narcissistic injury" is key to avoiding conflict.

In the minds of narcissistic people- both healthy and extreme- they are competent, have unique and special talents, and accomplished. In the case of healthy narcissists, any reasonable threat or challenge to these self-beliefs can be handled carefully, objectively, and in a proportionate way by the individual.

Threats to healthy narcissists don't include other successful or accomplished people- they may be positively competitive, but not derogatory. If a healthy narcissist takes a blow to their self-esteem, negative feelings may be processed without a melt-down or flying into a rage. Extreme narcissists, on the other hand, tend to exist in a world of hypervigilance. Any perceived threat or challenge is likely to be aggressively countered. Failing to do so could result in painful crashes to their self-esteem (narcissistic injury), as their opinion of themselves are overinflated, delicate and variable. This hypervigilance includes people they see as threatening, so it may be beneficial for you to lie low and purposely reduce the traits of your own that may make them feel competitive or badly about themselves.

Avoid Exposing Them

Exposing the narcissist and getting the "truth" out for all to see can be appealing and feel like the right thing to do. You may think this is the best solution for them, you and anyone else involved- that they will suddenly see clearly and take responsibility for changing their behavior. Forget about being right for a moment and bringing the truth to light.

Narcissists can Be extremely vindictive.

Pointing out that the narcissist is not as wonderful as think they are can result in a huge backlash, that you then must be around, and may not be able to escape. They are not ever going to agree with you, as they are tied to their elevated identity. Rather than changing their minds, they will be more likely to simply despise you for your opinions.

Narcissists can also be extremely vindictive. If you burst their bubble, they will regroup, and may well come back to make you pay. They may "rally the troops" and loyal fans that they have and turn others against you through whatever means they see necessary. If the narcissist is in a position of power over you, this can be an especially dangerous place to be.

Admire and Listen to Them

Being amenable is probably the most passive technique that you can take, but so long as you are not already on the narcissist's "naughty list" can be really effective at pulling you through difficult times, until you reach calmer waters or are able to end the relationship. Clinical psychologist Al Bernstein suggests that remaining quiet and allowing the narcissist to come up with reasons to congratulate themselves is easy, effortless and requires nothing more than listening and looking interested.

Admiring them, their achievements and qualities as much as they do can be a fast route into their "good books." So long as you avoid getting too close, this position in their good books can allow you to maintain a happier status quo with the narcissist still in your life.

Don't Reject Them

Rejecting a narcissist, whether in reality or in their perception, is likely to make them feel incredibly hurt or angry- as it causes a deep narcissistic injury. A jilted lover may feel a great deal of pain when the source of their affection no longer wants them. So, too, a narcissist feels deeply aggrieved when a source of narcissistic supply- or anyone else for that matter- decides that they are not "good enough."

Extreme narcissists – ever hypervigilant- may feel rejected for reasons that more average people would not. Being too busy or not having a good enough reason to deny their request for your company or collaboration can easily be taken to heart and result in an unexpectedly intense response. It's best to give them a legitimate reason that is beyond your control than to show that you're choosing to reject them. Being too busy to meet or see them is best if your reason is irrefutable, like having to work late to meet a specific deadline, attend an important wedding, or are booked onto a vacation or trip elsewhere.

Avoid Showing Weaknesses or Needs

If you show a narcissist what it is that makes you vulnerable, or what it is that you really want, they may at some point use it against you when they want to manipulate you. Narcissists will frequently learn what it is that you want most from them, and set about denying it so that you are in a constant state of "need." If a narcissistic mother does this, she may control her children through their neediness for her love. The same goes for a romantic partner. They'll ration your supply of what you enjoy most from them to keep you controllable and pliable.

If they know your greatest concerns or fears they may leverage these to manipulate you. They may even use you as a distraction from their own inner turmoil when they are experiencing crashing self-esteem, by needling you on your points of weakness, to make themselves feel strong again.

For example, an NPD manager suffering a meltdown of anxiety after a disastrous sales pitch may proceed to milk his staff for reassurance on his performance, whilst then moving the conversation on to subjects that he knows are extremely personal and emotional for them- transferring his fears to them and feeling better himself.

By not conceding any weaknesses to a narcissist and always taking a diplomatic "I know I'll be happy either way" approach, their power to bring you down whilst raising themselves higher is lost. This may take on the appearance of a game of cat and mouse, until eventually the narcissist must concede that you are not "easily pinned" or risk exposing themselves and being seen as a pessimistic and negative person.

Give Them an "Out" When They Attack

You can give them the opportunity to stop playing manipulative games by offering them an "out" such as: "You're being uncharacteristically pessimistic today- you're usually such an optimist- is there anything wrong?" and in doing so call them to return to their "higher state of glory" without continuing their attack. Subconsciously, they may even be aware that you successfully navigated their manipulation and decide to give you a wider berth in future, or that they need to keep you on side.

If the attack is particularly vicious or nasty, avoiding emotions but maintaining a cool, calm and empathic approach can work well to bring them back around. Whether you believe it or not, providing them with a defense that effectively excuses their behavior will be much appreciated - as it helps them to avoid a crushing sense of shame and subsequent denial loops, and simply feel that they are understood and forgiven. You may even be surprised to find that this approach results in a voluntary concession and what may seem like the beginnings or a more responsible approach, but this is not something that should be anticipated or expected.

Don't Expect Fairness

Extreme narcissists are likely to be far more concerned with getting what they want, than ensuring that everyone is treated fairly. Reward their behavior rather than their words so that they only get what they want, when you get what you want too.

Extending credit or accepting promises from an extreme narcissist is a dangerous leap of faith that may not be rewarded. Lack of follow through is just as likely to occur because the narcissist forgets their agreements- their attention being consumed with themselves and their own concerns rather than remembering their obligations. Make sure that you get what they promise before you give them what they want. A quid pro quo approach may be insulting to some people, but to a narcissist they are likely to respect you for looking out for yourself.

Know That They Want to Look Good

Understanding what a narcissist wants means that so long as you avoid triggering narcissistic injury, they may be able to be worked with. You may even be able to maneuver them, if you start to think like them.

Extreme narcissists really want to look good. If you can align what they want with what you want, you may be able to achieve great successes together. Alternatively, you may simply be able to manage and placate them to make your life easier or until you are able to leave the relationship.

Giving an extreme narcissist a way to be impressive if they do as they are told makes them easier to deal with, so long as you ensure you get what you want up front.

Understand Their Narcissistic Supply

Narcissists need people to gain narcissistic supply. You might compare that a healthier person needs others for mutual love and support, but as we proceed higher up the extreme narcissism scale, the need becomes more one-directional and desperate in nature, to prevent painful relapses to a place of low self-esteem. So, what exactly do they want from you?

Highly narcissistic people often prioritize relationships and career choices based on how much praise or attention they can receive. Many narcissistic people hamper their own development (or never develop a range of interests in the first place), by making choices for praise and success over other forms of enjoyment. If they have chosen you as a part of their life, it may be that you provide a high level of narcissistic supply.

Enthusiasm, love, caring and kindness are often qualities they look for in others. The amount and availability of "supply," unsurprisingly, takes precedence over other qualities like family responsibility, shared interests, complimentary personalities, or mutual concern for each other. If you have not been chosen voluntarily, you may find that your relationship quality depends on how readily give narcissistic supply, or whether you question or criticize them.

Bear in mind that narcissists are essentially addicts to narcissistic supply. They suffer crashes when they are unable to feed their habit and ramp up the search for supply to feel sustained. Any situation in which a narcissist is treated as different from ordinary people in their chosen way is likely to further damage them, encouraging them to further pursue the ego-feeding systems they already have in place.

This means that although you may identify their chosen sources of supply, and subtly use these to ensure that you do not become the addict's next victim, it should not be your intent to "love bomb" or swamp the narcissist with supply, as in doing so you are effectively harming them. If you feel that it's wrong to stand outside the gates of a school pedaling crack or selling bottles of alcohol to children until they are hooked, then you should think twice before flooding a narcissist with their drug of choice.

Taking responsibility for not damaging their wellbeing- whilst protecting your own- is as important for them as it is for anyone else. You would not feel great about filling the liquor cabinet in the home of an alcoholic, nor should you feel great about pedaling exorbitant approval and attention onto this already dependent individual. Moderate and considerate amounts to avoid attack or denigration is enough for you to get by.

An Audience
Narcissists often want an audience. They may spend a great deal of time talking about themselves. This serves their need to feel special (since they are always the subject of the discussion). They also get to let other people know how much they have accomplished in life. And the result of this is that they get lots of praise from other people.

Status
Presuming they don't feel threatened by people of high status, they may want to associate with them in order to feel superior to others. If you think you classify as "high status," this may be what they are using you for. In this case- check your own score for narcissism. It is not unknown for narcissists to flock together and form superficial friendships and relationships to "show off" to others and highlight

how special they both are, such as in a "trophy" partner / wealthy-partner relationship. Alternatively, they may want company from someone who is lower than they are to compare to themselves to, for a similar sense of superiority.

Some may choose a mix of friends- a bunch of successful equals to go out and "show off" with, and one or two best friends to feel superior to, to impress and revel in their attention.

When "lower level" friends have successes in their lives, the extreme narcissist may seem to visibly shrivel in comparison- feeling threatened rather than happy for their friends. Extreme narcissists may subconsciously think along the lines of: "How could this low-level person have such a success in comparison to me? Does this mean that I look like the worthless underdog in comparison to my low-level friend?" By comparison healthy narcissists will revel in the successes of their friends, feeling genuine joy and pleasure for them.

On the other hand, glorious successes in the lives of "higher level" friends may be bragged about and reveled in, almost as if they belong to the narcissist themselves, being used to reflect a higher status and level of achievement.

Sex
It may be that the extreme narcissist does not engage in sexual relationships for the emotional value it has; but for sex, and sex alone. They may revel in their ability to seduce, in their sexual performance, or in a sense of higher status or dominance within the sexual dynamic.

Love

Narcissistic people like to feel that there is someone who loves them and wants to be with them. Depending on how they view themselves, this may result in higher levels of infidelity or cheating. If a narcissist defines themselves as "good" or "moral" then cheating itself (or engaging in any generally scorned upon activities) could result in crushing shame and self-loathing, making it less likely to happen. On the other hand, if the narcissist is reluctant to see their partner as an equal, the likelihood of cheating increases.

Avoid Flooding them with Supply

If you are concerned about providing a narcissist with supply, keeping them in line can be aligned more with what they don't want. Being all about appearances, narcissists feel more shame than guilt. They really don't want to look bad.

Asking them to consider their reputation may make them think far more carefully than asking them to consider other people's feelings. If they think their actions will be perceived badly by others, they are far less likely to act. This can be achieved by asking them what people would think about what they did or asking probing questions to trigger them into having an alternative idea themselves.

Focusing on disappointment and emphasizing community rather than negotiating on points or becoming angry can help to change their choices. Help them to look good through doing good. Encouraging empathy by looking at why others could be disappointed by their actions -after they have first considered the damage to their reputation- may help them develop a more considerate approach up front.

-6-

What Happens Next

Handling an unhealthy/extreme narcissist is not an easy task, whether you choose to walk away or remain engaged in their lives to some degree.

If you decide to walk away and cut contact, how you handle this move is an important consideration. For non-abusive narcissists, being empathetic and considerate ensures that you can walk away feeling positive about your actions. Remember, the narcissist is unable to empathize at times, and this is often due to increased emotional sensitivity. Letting them down gently without confrontation or exposing them may be the kindest route to prevent them suffering a major blow to their self-esteem. However, in relationships where abuse is present, it may be advisable to cut the relationship swiftly, or in whatever way is safe and expedient for you.

When the Narcissist Returns

Like any person involved in a relationship, it is likely that the narcissist will at some point think of you and contact you. Depending on your relationship and the individual, they may be very hurt, angry or suspicious about why you are no longer involved with them. This may be understandably so.

For example, if you decided to stop speaking to a parent because their actions were detrimental to your well-being- their parental love for you (whether hidden or clearly displayed) will not simply disappear. It is claimed by many that narcissists do not love, but this is rarely the case, and only applicable at the very upper limits of the scale. It is more likely that they are unable to express or show their love in the presence of other people. Many narcissists find that their loving feelings become apparent when they emerge temporarily from the grips of their addiction to narcissistic supply.

They may contact you in a caring, human manner, to gloat, or in a manipulative attempt to reel you back in and gain something they want from you. Each situation, like each individual, is different. When possible, in response to these contact attempts, empathy is advisable, but delivered in a way that does not invite hope, questions or doubt. Be firm and stand by what you know is best, rather than being open to what they may offer you.

For example, if you have left a relationship with an emotionally abusive narcissist you may find that they contact you again in the future. Refusing contact is advisable, rather than discussing or reasoning with them, as no good can come from the interaction, only further harm. If they increase their attempts to contact you, become angry, emotional or abusive, a strict attitude of no reaction can eventually force them to gain control of themselves and move on.

However, if you have been keeping your distance from a non-abusive family member- with unhealthy but not overwhelming narcissistic tendencies- you might welcome the opportunity to have a positive and well-meaning conversation. This does not mean that you are opening yourself up for dangerous or pre-emptive closeness, but simply means that you are experimenting with being present in their lives, so long as they are able to behave in a reasonable manner. If they are still unable to behave well, then you may decide whether you want to continue the relationship or increase the distance further.

How to Stop Someone Being a Narcissist

Essentially, if someone is being unhealthily narcissistic, it is up to them to notice and correct their behavior, rather that anyone else to point it out to them and risk the backlash from a narcissistic injury. Healthy narcissism may work well, but it is important that it does not develop into a dependence on approval and attention to an extreme degree in the long term.

Highly narcissistic people are usually unaware that they are so, as they live very often in a state of denial and are unlikely to attempt to improve or work on themselves. In some cases, suspecting or being diagnosed with having NPD can provide significant motivation for people to change, as was found by Dr Craig Malkin of Harvard medical school. During online discussions on identifying narcissism he found the most distressed and heartfelt pleas for help and advice on how to improve came not from people in the lives of narcissists, but from those that had been diagnosed with or suspected they had NPD.

Happily, he believes that narcissists are able to change the ways in which they see the world, but that this rarely happens. This is because in the case of narcissists, many will live, perpetually unaware or in denial of their skewed lens, and will never attempt to improve it.

Although we cannot condemn those that want to change with a sentence of "irrevocably permanent narcissism" - for change to happen a person has to *want* to change and be capable of facing the work necessary to make improvements. It is *no one else's* responsibility to make this happen but the person who is overly narcissistic themselves. This means, that if you are caught up in the life of a narcissist, whether you decide to make them aware of your suspicions or not, nothing can make them improve, unless they decide that they are ready to do so. This decision may come at a point of desperation, and real progress- if it comes at all- may take many years to solidify.

To overcome narcissism, a first step is to recognize the role of addiction to narcissistic supply and stop attempting to secure it. Accepting that being ordinary is okay is essential, and that no matter what successes or failures life brings- a person can never become more than just a person- equal to everyone else. The urge to stand out from the crowd needs to be quashed.

If it's impossible to stop supplying the ego- - then aligning this need with a positive cause can at least make a difference in the world. Like any addiction, fighting it can be extremely difficult, and overcoming it whilst still being intoxicated is highly unlikely to happen. Rather than fighting to remain in control of narcissism, the narcissist must take responsibility for starving it and going "cold turkey," as with any alcoholic or drug addict.

-7-

Assessing the Situation Objectively

You may be fully aware that you are a source of narcissistic supply, a target for manipulation, or abusive behavior. Perhaps it is clear that you must either break off or continue the relationship. But for those who are still in the questioning phase, unsure about what is happening and the extent to which they need to act, there are several exercises you can do to help you see more clearly.

Abuse Checklist

Extreme narcissistic people may be abusive if they are unhealthy enough, as they may be unable to be empathic to others. If you're unsure as to whether you're involved in an abusive interaction, take a look at the following checklist. Many victims of abuse live in a state of denial regarding the true nature of the situation, making justifications for their loved ones and excusing their abusive behavior. Abuse can be an insidious process that can leave the victim feeling confused and upset for an extended period after it has finished. It can have crippling effects on the victim's sense of self-worth and confidence and should not be ignored or allowed to continue after it has been identified.

There are various types of abuse- emotional/psychological, sexual, physical and financial/material. As a summary, you have the right to emotional support in your relationships, be heard by your partner, and be responded to with courtesy. You also have the right to have your feelings and experiences acknowledged as real and valid, clear and informative answers to questions that concern you, to live free from criticism and judgment, live free from accusation and blame. You should receive encouragement, live free from emotional and physical threat and be respectfully asked to do things rather than "ordered." You should receive goodwill from your partner   and   live free from angry outbursts and rage.

Each type of abuse has various indicators split out in the lists that follow. If you're unsure about whether you are experiencing abuse, identify which indicators apply to your relationship with the person in question. Multiple indicators mean that it is more likely that what you are experiencing classifies as abuse.

Emotional abuse

Emotional abuse can be difficult to identify objectively. Knowing where to draw the line between regular disagreements, strong personalities, victim mentality and genuine abusive behavior can be difficult.

Has the person in question shown the following characteristics, in an abusive manner:

- called you offensive names
- ridiculed your beliefs, religion, race, class or sexual orientation
- strongly criticized or threatened to hurt your family or friends
- kept you away from family and friends
- abused animals
- was unreasonably angry if you paid too much attention to someone or something else (children, friends, job, etc.)
- withheld approval, appreciation or affection, more than would be considered part of a normal argument within your cultural context
- humiliated you

- become angry if meals or housework were not done to their liking, more than would be considered part of a normal argument within your cultural context
- made contradictory demands / changed the rules in order to confuse you
- did not include you in important decisions, more than would be considered part of a normal argument within your cultural context
- purposely did not allow you to sleep
- harassed you or threatened to tell others about things you have done in the past
- taken away car keys, money or credit cards
- checked up on you (listened to your phone calls, looked at phone bills, checked car mileage, etc.) more than would be considered part of a normal situation within your cultural context
- degraded you
- made you feel insignificant, powerless and/or worthless
- threatened to commit suicide
- interfered with your work or school (provoked a fight in the morning, harass you at work, etc.)
- embarrassed or humiliated you in front of other people
- abused your children

- used drugs or alcohol to excuse their behavior
- used phrases like "I'll show you who's boss," "I'll put you in line"
- used a loud or intimidating tone of voice, more than would be considered part of a normal argument within your cultural context
- criticized your body, weight, clothes, or other aspects of your appearance, more than would be considered normal within your cultural context

Sexual abuse

Has the person in question:
- significantly pressured you to have sex, or given you inappropriate, unwanted sexual attention, more than would be considered normal within your cultural context
- pressured you to perform sexual acts that made you uncomfortable or hurt you, more than would be considered normal within your cultural context
- directed physical injury toward sexual areas of your body
- put you at risk for unwanted pregnancy or sexually transmitted diseases
- withheld sex or affection

- used sexual terms as insults
- accused you of having or wanting sex with others
- forced you to have sex with others
- forced you to view pornography
- pressured you to dress in a certain way, more than would be considered part of a normal argument within your cultural context
- disregarded your sexual needs and feelings about sex (for heterosexual relationships)
- accused you of being gay if you refused sex
- spread rumors about your sexual behaviors
- made you or refused to let you use birth control
- made unwanted public sexual advances
- made remarks about your sexual abilities
- sexually assaulted or raped you

Physical abuse

Has the person in question:

- pushed, grabbed or shoved you
- slapped you
- punched you
- kicked you

- choked you
- pinched you
- pulled your hair
- burned you
- bit you
- tied you up
- forced you to share needles with others
- threatened you with a knife, gun or other weapon
- used a knife, gun or other weapon
- prevented you from leaving an area / physically restrained you
- thrown objects
- destroyed property, possessions or important documents
- drove recklessly to frighten you
- disregarded your needs when you were ill, injured or pregnant
- abused you while you were pregnant
- forced you to abort or carry a pregnancy

Financial abuse

Has the person in question:

- made all the decisions about money

- taken care of all financial matters without your input
- criticized the way or amounts of money you spent
- placed you on a budget that was unrealistic
- denied you access to bank accounts and credit cards
- refused to put your name on joint assets
- controlled your paycheck
- refused you access to money
- refused to let you work
- refused to get a job
- caused you to lose your job

Having read through the checklists above, if you think you may have been the victim of abuse and need to get help escaping or leaving a situation, please see a list of resources at the end of this book for people living in the US and UK. Similar resources may be available in other countries by Googling "abuse services" in the local language.

Logbook of Events

Sometimes it is difficult to assess a situation when you are in the midst of it. Keeping a log book of interactions, arguments or alarming events can really help to see a relationship more objectively over time, to assess the severity and cause of any problems. The exercise below is an example of how you might structure a logbook entry:

Day/date:

Type of Event:

Event trigger from your point of view:

Event trigger from the other person's point of view:

What happened from your point of view:

What happened from the other person's point of view:

Was there a narcissistic or overreaction involved on their part? If yes, what was it?

Being honest, was there a narcissistic or overreaction involved on your part? If yes, what was it?

Was there any element of abuse present in the other person's behavior, and any present in your behavior? (See checklist on what constitutes abuse above)

What would an objective third party think about the trigger of the event?

What would an objective third party think about what happened if they had witnessed the whole event?

What would an objective third party advise you to do if they had seen the event?

Assessing a Narcissist's Triggers

Assessing a narcissist and what makes them tick can be extremely useful in determining how to best handle them. Depending on your goals, whether these be to survive, thrive, or peacefully co-exist, learning their triggers can make the difference between peace and fury.

If you decide not to walk away, it might be an idea to consider purposely becoming less threatening. Avoiding triggering their insecurities, areas of competition, and knowing how to make them feel appreciated can help you to avoid storms and navigate through the waves.

Being true to yourself, is always preferable to pretending to be something that you are not. However, you may be able to find a compromise, that does not threaten the narcissist, whilst still being true to yourself in important ways. Whatever works for you. For example, self-deprecating humor is consistently applied by the British to make others feel comfortable and to appear non-threatening. Being able to laugh at yourself can put many people at ease. This does not compromise any values of "being true to oneself" as being able to make fun of your flaws is a modest and positive quality.

If you choose to go further, you can avoid talking about (or even downplay) the talents, characteristics and experiences you possess that you think the narcissist will find threatening and emphasizing your interests and hobbies that they find non-threatening. If you must interact with them, this may be preferable rather than risk invoking their fury and attempts to control or undermine you. It is not a perfect solution, but it is your choice to decide how you need to behave to get what you would like from the situation. Remember that you are attempting to avoid conflict rather than to create it.

Below you will find a guided exercise to assess the narcissist, to help you handle them in the future.

What does the narcissist believe their talents to be?

Is the narcissist competitive in any of these talents?

Have you identified any triggers for insecurity within the narcissist?

What does the narcissist consider to be "non-threatening" in others? I.e. What talents, subjects etc. do not cross-over into their "realms of importance" in which they need control? Are you heavily involved in any non-threatening areas? These may become safe subjects to have non-threatening conversations about.

Achieving Independent Coexistence in a Group

You might be operating in an environment where a narcissist (or several) holds all the cards in your family, career, or friendship group, and you would like to adjust the dynamics. This could be the difference between being able to remain within the group, without being damaged, used or controlled, and having to walk away. The new dynamic could even work out as beneficial for everyone.

Being non-threatening and independent in the same group as a narcissist can be tricky to achieve, as narcissists tend to be paranoid and generally concerned by anybody they can't control. If you decide not to walk away, and that remaining means more to you than leaving, it can be helpful to understand the group dynamics, before packaging yourself as a harmless character.

Harmless characters can usually exist outside the paranoid boundaries and control that is applied to everybody else. Understanding what the narcissist finds threatening, entertaining and complimentary can be extremely helpful when deciding how best to "repackage" yourself- if this is what you want to do.

Below you'll find an exercise sheet to help you assess what to do next:

Who is / are the narcissists in the group:

Is / are there any enablers within the group (enablers are passive but well-meaning types who allow the narcissists to continue with their bad behavior by not confronting it):

Are there any sources of narcissistic supply within the group? Are you one?

Are there any regular victims of the narcissist?

How does the narcissist control the group, and you in particular?

Why does the narcissist feel superior?

What does the narcissist find threatening in general, and about you in particular?

Are there any subjects, hobbies or things that the narcissist admires without finding them threatening? (e.g. Humor, political activities, a different kind of style, an alternative lifestyle etc.) Do you have an interest in any of these?

How can you use this insight to help you achieve your goal of peaceful coexistence within the group?

-8-

Final Word

As we've seen, misconceptions of narcissism as a black and white "thing" that people either "are," or "are not" is an oversimplified approach.

Narcissism exists on a scale of self-enhancement, with too little, healthy levels, and extreme levels. Unhealthy or extreme narcissism increases as dependence on narcissistic supply increases. Individuals with extreme or unhealthy traits may have underlying self-esteem issues which promote the appeal of narcissistic supply, helping to propagate the addiction, although this is not always the case.

Using the addiction model, we see that people who are dependent on narcissistic supply are "gripped" by narcissism and may act in ways that are extremely detrimental- even abusive- to those around them to maintain the one-directional flow of approval to keep themselves inflated. Rather than fighting to remain in control of narcissism, the narcissist must take responsibility for starving it – perhaps going cold turkey, as an alcoholic or drug addict may choose to do. A narcissist must accept that being ordinary is acceptable and relinquish the drive to stand out as superior from the rest of humanity.

In the long-run, narcissists are unhappy, and make those around them unhappy, meaning that the best option when dealing with a narcissist who is not undergoing a period of self-enlightenment or change (which is highly unlikely in this group), is to cut off or limit contact, depending on the nature of your relationship. As some narcissists are vulnerable to varying self-esteem, and hypervigilant to the slightest insult or threat they may be very sensitive to narcissistic injury. In these cases, the narcissist may become abusive to a degree that even a distant relationship is not possible.

If cutting contact from a narcissist is not possible, other techniques may be employed to make life easier, and avoid infuriating or upsetting them. Avoiding being in their inner circle, whilst remaining warm and approving allows a safe distance to be maintained- making attack or upset far less likely. Causing unnecessary injury to their ego through exposing them as abusive or less than they think themselves to be, rejecting them or outshining them is likely to backfire and cause a great deal of commotion. If peace is the main objective, understanding and avoiding these triggers is preferable.

Making sure that a narcissist delivers on what they may tempt you with, rather than expecting fairness and extending credit, is particularly important when negotiating. Narcissists want to look good and understanding this is the key to channeling them in the right direction, without flooding them with narcissistic supply.

Caution is needed when deciphering what type of narcissistic supply is desired by a narcissist. Flooding them with this or any other attention that makes them feel overly special is likely to further their addiction, as well as draw you into their dangerous inner circle. Remember that you are dealing with a complicated human being, with their own battles to fight, just as you have yours. As dramatic as it sounds, offering up a great deal of narcissistic supply to someone whose well-being is dependent on it may in fact be as morally questionable as supplying an alcoholic or drug addict with a narcotic. Be balanced and fair, without flooding them, when you are able.

Finally, and most importantly, it is our ultimate responsibility to ensure that a narcissist is not able to damage us or our dependents, and that in withdrawing or protecting ourselves we do not damage the narcissist- if possible. The "securing your own oxygen mask" before helping to secure another's scenario on a plane is a good analogy for where our responsibilities should lie- despite narcissists attempts to make you take care of their needs before your own. Leaving an abusive situation should be considered to have the utmost urgency (abuse services can be found in the following pages).

However, handling a sensitive or manipulative person who is non-abusive, should be done so through the lens of someone who can see the humanity of the people involved. Whilst you do not need to have undue sympathy or empathy for a damaging individual, this does not give you free reign to behave badly in return.

Your priority is to manage the situation for the good of yourself and your dependents first, but also for everyone that is involved. If the situation cannot be managed well, it may be best to walk away and disengage.

Abuse Services

US:

- Center against domestic violence: http://www.cadvny.org
- National Domestic Violence Helpline: www.thehotline.org

UK:

- NHS Abuse services: www.nhs.uk/Livewell/abuse/Pages/domestic-violence-help.asp
- Domestic violence support: www.refuge.org.uk

Bibliography

1. Meta-analysis: "Impulsivity and the Self-Defeating Behavior of Narcissists." Personality and Social Psychology Review (2006).

2. "Examining the Relations Among Narcissism, Impulsivity, and Self-Defeating Behaviors." Journal of Personality (2009).

3. "Narcissism as Addiction to Esteem." Psychological Inquiry (2001).

4. "The Narcissist You Know: Defending Yourself Against Extreme Narcissists in an All-About-Me Age." New York: Touchstone (2016).

5. "Psychology Research Breakthrough Suggests Narcissists are Capable of Empathy" University of Surrey (2016). https://www.surrey.ac.uk/features/psychology-research-breakthrough-suggests-narcissists-are-capable-empathy

6. "New Insights into Narcissistic Personality Disorder" Psychiatric Times Special Reports, DSM-5 (2016). http://www.psychiatrictimes.com/special-reports/new-insights-narcissistic-personality-disorder

7. "Fear and decision making in narcissistic personality disorder" Dialogues in Clinical Narcissism (2013). https://www.ncbi.nlm.nih.gov/pmc/articles/PMC3811090/#ref7

ABOUT THE AUTHOR

Okay, okay, the secret's out... Amazon best-selling author, 'Theresa Jackson,' is a pen name. The alternative identity of a popular investigative author, she's exploring sensitive issues like family, grief and relationships, without the risk of bring her nearest and dearest into the spotlight.

Theresa has a Master's degree in clinical research and a Bachelor's degree in physics with astrophysics. She spent half of her childhood in the Bahamas before returning to England, studying and traveling the world. After several years spent working in South Korea, Spain, and the Netherlands, Theresa returned to London where she worked for five years serving pharmaceutical companies in healthcare marketing and advertising agencies. Now living in Italy, she works as a writer, and applies her restless mind to answering burning questions using scientific evidence and a human touch.

Don't you just wish you could say what you really think? Join 'Theresa,' and let it out. Jump on the exploration freight train and get a greater understanding of yourself and others.

Follow Theresa's work at theresa-jackson.com where you can sign up to her newsletter.

Books by Theresa Jackson

How to Handle a Narcissist

Loss of a Parent, Adult Grief when Parents Die (excerpt follows)

"Stepping Away from a Narcissist Kit" is a workbook made to accompany this book, and is available for purchase on Amazon or as a free download at theresa-jackson.com

Future Work

"In future I'll be diving into how to build emotional resilience and follow your dreams. A step by step guide to jumping off the metaphorical cliff and setting your sights on happiness.

If you would like to know when the next book is ready or to be kept informed of special offers, freebies and giveaways, email me at theresa.jackson.books@gmail.com and I'll add you to my readers list.

Theresa."

Leave A Review...

If you enjoyed this book, found it useful or otherwise then I'd really appreciate it if you would post a short review on Goodreads, Amazon, Barnes and Noble, iTunes or wherever you purchased the book. I do read all the reviews personally so that I can continually write what people are wanting.

Excerpt from:

Loss of A Parent
Adult Grief When Parents Die

I lost my father at the end of 2007, from a heart attack, which is the reason I decided to write this book. Eighteen months earlier he had suffered a debilitating stroke that left him a virtual vegetable in a bed. Slowly and painstakingly he had fought for recovery and was immensely happy to be alive. He had reached the point of being able to live a mobile, happy life, only to be lost unexpectedly.

But just like that, he was gone. The fact that I would never be able to see him or talk to him again, even if just to say goodbye was something I didn't want to face.

Although I cannot know your personal circumstances, or where your emotional journey will take you, I can start by saying sorry for your loss. I'm sorry that you find yourself in this most horrible of clubs that nobody ever wants to join. And I can reassure you that you are not alone in what you are going through.

There are various recognized states during grief, but despite this the process of grieving is different for everybody. We'll be looking at many different people's stories, to give you an idea that different reactions and grief pathways are to be expected, and no two people are the same when dealing with grief.

Made in the USA
San Bernardino, CA
01 August 2020